THE POSITIVE USE OF COMMERCIAL TELEVISION WITH CHILDREN

by *Rosemary Lee Potter*

Produced in cooperation
with
NEA Instruction and Professional Development

National Education Association
Washington, D.C.

Note
The opinions expressed in this publication should not be construed as representing the policy or position of the National Education Association. Materials published as part of the Analysis and Action Series are intended to be discussion documents for teachers who are concerned with specialized interests of the profession.

Acknowledgment
Channel Chuckles, by Bil Keane, reprinted courtesy The Register and Tribune Syndicate.

Library of Congress Cataloging in Publication Data

Potter, Rosemary Lee.
  The positive use of commercial television with children.

  (Analysis and action series)
  Reprint. Originally published: New season.
Columbus, Ohio: Merrill, c1976.
  Bibliography: p.
  Includes index.
    1. Television and children. 2. Television in education. 3. Television broadcasting — Social aspects. I. Title.   II. Series.
HQ784.T4P68   1981   305.2'3   81–9646
ISBN 0–8106–1686–6   AACR2

The Author
Rosemary Lee Potter, a former classroom teacher, is a middle school Reading Specialist with the Pinellas County Schools, Clearwater, Florida. Dr. Potter, the parent of twin teenagers, is the author of research, books, classroom materials, educational articles, and a syndicated newspaper column on the use of television with children.

Contents

Fine Tuning

WHAT IS POSITIVE USE?

One of the best ways to offset the difficulties TV poses to children is to intervene in their viewing process by making constructive use of the massive TV experience in question.

WHAT IS COMMERCIAL TELEVISION?

Commercial television is specifically those television programs which school-aged children choose to watch at home and which generally have a commercial sponsor. Due to space limitations, this book excludes detailed consideration of public, educational, and cable television.

It's About Prime Time

If you are already certain that commercial television today has in itself little positive value for children, this book, I hope, will not change your mind. I agree with you. I shout hooray for citizen's groups such as Action for Children's Television (ACT) which, as advocates for young people, are having some effect in diminishing the excesses of commercial TV.

While there is some evidence of slight improvement, the fact remains, however, that millions of children watched five or more hours this very day—watched TV just as it is. The news is that we who teach them and who care for them can intervene in their television scene, using their beloved medium to help them learn.

There are some hopeful signs of change. Many teachers have reported classroom use of TV as a valuable resource, according to **Today's Education** (see source list). During the last five years almost every educational publication of consequence has devoted some space to the idea that TV can be harnessed to a variety of positive teaching strategies. New publications providing information and research, such as **Television and Children,** have emerged. This book has the same purpose. First published in 1976 by Charles E. Merrill Publishing Company, now in a new NEA edition it offers teachers a challenge to check out TV as a frontier teaching and learning tool. To help you get started I have included (1) an introductory summary of recent developments in school TV use; (2) a source list to facilitate the use of strategies; (3) the reasons for TV's continuing promise for innovative educational researchers; (4) a report of four early research projects which used commercial TV to assist and assess children's reading and thinking; (5) a group of unique and productive TV-related experiences, classroom-tested in language arts, reading, social studies, and other curriculum areas, at varying levels; (6) an assessment of the still-emerging trend of interest in the use of commercial TV; and (7) a reference list of sources spanning a 22-year period.

The activities in this book neither approve present TV fare nor encourage more extensive viewing. In many instances, however, specific programs are mentioned—some current, some in reruns, and some long gone from the screen. These shows were selected not for promotion, but for their long-standing popularity and value to the particular lesson to be taught. Each serves as a prototype source, an idea starter. The activities are designed to capitalize on the wealth of data and TV viewing experiences students **already have,** turning it to studies they must address.

It is my hope, then, that as you read this book, you will decide to join me in studying and using commercial television to help children learn regular classroom lessons. I assure you that this sort of decision and scrutiny has its consequences. It raises one's level of TV awareness. It helps one become more critical. TV-related instruction has provided me and many other teachers with a special professional expertise in touch with the here an now—a prime key to successful contemporary teaching.

Sources for the materials and ideas discussed below are listed at the end of this introductory section and on the back cover of this book.

Television and Schools: What's Going On?

THE BOOK CONNECTION

The most splendid development in television use in schools continues to be a very traditional and staple item—tie-in books. Researchers, publishers, teachers, and librarians alike increasingly attest to the way that television is directly motivating many children—to read.

During the late 70's and early 80's all three commercial television networks encouraged the TV-reading connection with official book tie-in projects. Now each network often bases distinguished programming on distinguished writing. Certainly this is great public relations. It is also a fabulous windfall for tuned-in teachers.

SCRIPTS: A FRESH LOOK AT PLAYREADING

Since I first wrote about TV scriptreading over a decade ago, such reading projects have flourished with millions of youngsters now reading the teleplays of popular TV shows. Television scripts with teacher-written guides are sold and distributed by networks and private firms, included in textbooks, and published in their entirety or as excerpts by newspapers. From reading and, especially, from classroom observation, my colleagues and I notice certain results when using TV scripts—now absentee rates, high attention spans, sincere interest in discussing motivation and details, and, best of all, high scores in applied specific reading skills and vocabulary taken from the scripts.

CRITICAL VIEWING SKILLS

In the late 70's the Office of Education (OE) stimulated a nationwide interest in teaching youngsters to be more critical in their television watching. Among many objectives, government educators announced that children should be able to distinguish between TV formats—for instance, between programs and commercials—and to understand the nature of the persuasive advertising techniques directed at them. By 1980 many new critical viewing skills materials were available from the OE groups, private firms, and universities. These include filmstrips, viewing logs, worktexts, read-to booklets, textbooks, manuals, videotapes, and even a do-while-viewing game aimed at promoting judicious TV use or TV literacy.

Additional critical viewing skills projects include one in Idaho which teaches children to make critical judgments about TV they "receive" and an ABC-sponsored Yale University project for third to fifth graders which uses research-based videotapes and software geared to develop close examination and understanding of TV. Other educators and curriculum designers have integrated the critical study of video with the critical study of print. If children identify the main idea in a newspaper article, textbook, or short story, why not do the same with a TV program? Prime-Time School TV has long subscribed to this idea, continuing to supply teachers and parents with in-depth secondary units of TV-related study—concepts such as the selection and content of news, principles of economics and distortion, applied to video police work.

THE STUDENT TV-PRODUCTION ERA

Wherever students have the opportunity to use the video camera, they are producing their own learning materials. Such shows are usually teacher supervised, yet student designed and executed. This idea is quickly taking hold, with well-documented high learning levels and self-discipline.

Small school TV "stations" are also springing up around the country. For example, a Clearwater, Florida, middle school broadcasts a weekly student TV news program to the student body. At a Gaithersburg, Maryland, elementary school first graders sometimes anchor the school's TV station. A Title IV-C Video Curriculum Project in the Albuquerque Public Schools is encouraging teachers to use video through dynamic how-to tapes, seminars, and technical assistance.

THE TV-PARENTING TREND

Parents continue to be concerned with their children's inappropriate and gluttonous viewing. One has only to mention the subject of children and television to let loose a strong flood of worried parental anecdotes. Materials and suggestions from organized parental groups and from some media-supported firms may help. They seem promising.

PREVIEWS

What's next? Along comes videodisc—still another way to hook up with TV. Students who have loved the electronic game arcade and the small computers and VCRs moving into their schools are becoming fascinated by laser reading. A laser imprints 54,000 frames of school content on a silvery, nearly indestructible, disc. Then a laser beam situated in a player "reads" the material contained on it, displaying it on a TV screen. The NEA is producing SCHOOLDISC with ABC to teach basic school concepts—distributing it in a special curriculum package with a videodisc player and hours of videodiscs. The material in this program was written by classroom teachers.

Educators are also being asked to read pre-production scripts, to sit in on early planning of programs, to appear on panels about TV, to consult at conferences, and to plan interschool cable content. Furthermore, it appears likely that training in TV use will become part of teacher education.

WRAP-UP

I am **making the most of TV** at home and school. I have even used those boldfaced words as the title of a weekly column I write for several daily newspapers. Many people write to me. That's how I know that teachers and parents and grandparents and, above all, students are making an effort to manage TV in their lives and to learn from it and enjoy it. If you figure out some successful way to make TV work for your students, let other teachers know about it. You may never find another topic as fertile for study. That's the way it can be.

The Emmys

I wish to thank all the people who are helping me discover the positive possibilities of commercial television. Thousands of children and hundreds of teachers and parents have thus far participated in the experiences described in this book.

For their help and encouragement, I am particularly grateful to University of Miami (Florida) Professor of Education, Dr. Arnold B. Cheyney; to Miami principals James Reed, Dr. David Felton, Robert Maloney, and Dr. Paul Madsen; to Dr. Peggy Burgess, formerly of Florida Atlantic University (Boca Raton); and to Dr. Charles E. Hannemann, Assistant Professor of Education and Area Coordinator of Instructional Technology at the University of Miami.

I also thank my family—my husband, my twin sons, and my father.

Rosemary Lee Potter
Clearwater, Florida

SOURCES

GENERAL

Television and Children
National Council for Children and Television
20 Nassau Street, Suite 215
Princeton, NJ 08540

Kahn, Linda. "The Big Picture: NEA Involvement in TV." **Today's Education** (September-October 1980): 64-65SS.

TV AND BOOKS

Community Relations
ABC-TV
1330 Avenue of the Americas
New York, NY 10019

Read More About It
The CBS/Library of Congress Book Project
CBS, Inc.
51 West 52d Street
New York, NY 10019

NBC-TV
30 Rockefeller Plaza
New York, NY 10020

Potter, Rosemary Lee. "The Link Between Reading Instruction and Commercial Television: Is This a Bandwagon?" **Journal of Reading** (February 1981); 377-82.

Singer, Dorothy G. "Television Tie-Ins in the School Library." **School Library Journal** (September 1979); 51-52.

Unger, Arthur. "Why TV Won't Be Replacing Books." **Christian Science Monitor** (December 14, 1979).

TV SCRIPTS

CBS Television Reading Program (at above address)

The Television Reading Program
Capital Cities Communications, Inc.
4110 City Line Avenue
Philadelphia, PA 19131

Movie Scriptreader Program Films, Inc.
50 Rindge Avenue Extension
Cambridge, MA 02140

Scholastic Book Services
904 Sylvan Avenue
Englewood Cliffs, NJ 97632

Xerox Education Publications
1250 Fairwood Avenue
Columbus, OH 43216

Potter, Rosemary Lee. "An Interview with a Pioneer." **Teacher** (April 1978);
44-48.

CRITICAL VIEWING SKILLS

U.S. Office of Education Critical Viewing Skills Projects:

Elementary School
Soutwest Educational Development Laboratory (SEDL)
211 East 7th Street
Austin, TX 78701

Middle School
WNET, Channel 13
356 West 58th Street
New York, NY 10019

Secondary School
Far West Laboratory for Educational Research and Development
1855 Folsom Street
San Francisco, CA 94103

Postsecondary
Boston University School of Public Communication
640 Commonwealth Avenue
Boston, MA 02215

The Way We See It: Instruction in Critical Receivership
N. Craig Ashton
Idaho Falls School District #91
Idaho Falls, ID 83401

Rosemary M. Lehman
In Touch With . . .
5513 Thunderbird Lane
Monona, WI 53716

Getting the Most Out of Television
Drs. Jerome and Dorothy Singer
Yale University Family Television Research and Consultation Center
405 Temple Street
New Haven, CN 06511

Channel: Critical Reading/TV Viewing Skills and the TV Readers Skill Kit
Educational Activities, Inc.
P.O. Box 392
Freeport, NY 11520

Prime Time School Television
120 South LaSalle Street
Chicago, IL 60603

Cheyney, Arnold B., and Rosemary Lee Potter. **Video: A Handbook Showing the
Use of Television in the Elementary Classroom.** Stevensville, Mich.; Educational Service, Inc., 1980.

(Continued on back cover)

Why Not Football or Halloween?

In 1966 I completed a fascinating NDEA (National Defense Education Act) graduate school project in which children in first grade were involved with puppets in the hope of improving the youngsters' oral capabilities. The main topic of "talk" chosen by the children as they made puppets "speak" was television programs. In particular, the puppets often "narrated" adventures from the then televised "Batman" program. In addition to increased verbal output, I noted that reluctant children, who were otherwise experiencing difficulties in reading and language arts, became eager learners when asked to read brief stories about "Batman" self-dictated to the teacher. The children paid unusually close attention to detail, listened more closely to other readers, read complex sentences, and attacked unknown and difficult words with great confidence. So interested did the children appear to be in the television-related reading materials developed, that those experiencing difficulty were happy to receive coaching from peers and teacher. In all, the children were willing to read stories whose vocabulary was drawn from oral dictation far more difficult than class texts.

1

As the semester progressed, student teachers noted that EVERY child was involved in these television reading experiences by his or her own request. The obvious high interest led me to conjecture about this apparently dynamic use of commercial television. I guessed that since virtually every child was familiar with the "Batman" program and watched it at home by choice, the children transferred the interest drawn from it to use in school. If this were so, I reasoned, there may be other ways that I might "turn on" commercial television—to enhance children's learning.

Teacher-friends who learned about this application of commercial television immediately asked, "But why TV? With all its problems . . . why not football, pets, or hobbies, as a context for reading and thinking?" Years later, college educators would ask, "Why not fairy tales or special days such as Halloween? Aren't there dozens of other highly intriguing childhood experiences from which we can draw data to devise reading activities?"

TV AND CHILD-INTEREST

The answer to all the above questions is yes, of course. There are many childhood interests on which we have long relied for stimulation and motivation in reading, storywriting, and discussion. Dogs, dinosaurs, parties, vacations, and motorcycles, for example, will continue to supply stimulating data to motivate children's intentions toward learning. However, no less important is any other childhood interest that can be shown to be a forceful and common source of data and language stimulation. Commercial television programming is proving just such a powerful alternative, as shown by independent researchers examining its widespread and constant popularity with children.

Even if there were not research, which is treated in detail in chapter 3, in what topic other than commercial television can we claim so much investment of childhood time? What other interest can be said to be present daily, according to Lyle and Hoffman, in over 96 percent of American homes (p. 21)? To what other experience do we now, according to Savage, estimate that children devote a full day (24 hours) per week (p. 133)? Name any other children's experience with such commonality that almost all high school graduates can claim, according to Haney, over 15,000 hours of commitment during years of classroom time totaling only 11,000 hours (p. 51)?

Why Not Football or Halloween?

Although football and other sports still do not fascinate all girls, commercial television intensely interests most younger children of both sexes. As topics, pets and parties, hobbies, and the home interest various children to different degrees, but we are able to approach almost any given child with a foreknowledge of his or her interest in television programs. If we are determining the reading interests of the children we are helping, we fortunately find a variety of interests from which to draw to plan interesting stories. However, we need not hesitate to use any high-interest idea which might catch the attention of even the most reluctant child. Fairy tales are absorbing. It has been established that particular children, certain sexes, and varying-aged youngsters enjoy these old stories, but such tales do not have the year-long out-of-school interest of most children. Likewise, Halloween is super as a source of motivation for a day, a week, or at most, a month.

But again, why TV? The answer is that commercial television is a sustained interest of most children. If we really believe that we should employ child interest to help children learn, then commercial television must be recognized, included, and, above all, **used** to child advantage.

AMERICAN STUDIES OF TV

Aside from my own observations of the popularity of commercial television, large-scale research projects indicate the same findings I have noted from experience. Since 1950 home television has become a component of almost every child's daily life. At least three major studies—those of Witty and Kinsella; Schramm, Lyle, and Parker; and Lyle and Hoffman—revealed that commercial television programs are the objects of constant interest for American children. These comprehensive investigations were conducted to determine the nature and extent of televiewing by children.

In 1962 Witty and Kinsella compiled and summarized findings of a twelve-year study (1949–1962) using multi-aged children in Chicago. This compilation first established the constancy and commonality of televiewing among American children. Its authors also first reported the use of teacher-selected home television programs correlated with school work and suggested that one could learn from commercial television. Witty and Kinsella reported that second graders watched sixteen hours a week. Among the most frequently watched programs were "Three Stooges," "Flintstones," "Top Cat," "Dick Tracy," "Margie," and "Ben Casey" (pp. 779-802).

In 1961 Schramm, Lyle, and Parker conducted another study with a sample of 6,000 children in first, sixth, and tenth grades in the United States and Canada. These researchers were still able to compare nonwatchers with watchers—almost an impossibility today. Their conclusion was that the effect of such heavy televiewing on children depended entirely on "the way children use it" (p. 1).

Finally, in a study in 1971 paralleling the one just described, Lyle and Hoffman surveyed over 1,500 school children to collect data on television. The sample included many first-grade youngsters and first-grade mothers, over 800 sixth graders, and about 500 tenth graders. In general, Lyle and Hoffman found that a third of first graders watched television before school in the morning and that in the late afternoon peak viewing time, about two-thirds of first graders were watching. No significant differences were found in the amount of viewing by socioeconomic or major ethnic groups, Anglo- and Mexican-American. The small subsample of Afro-Americans manifested the heaviest viewing at each age level.

According to Lyle and Hoffman, the most popular commercial television programs among first graders were situation comedies and cartoon shows, the five most popular shows being "Gilligan's Island" (by far), "Flintstones," "Lucy," "My Favorite Martian," and "Batman" (pp. 3-7).

FOREIGN STUDIES OF TV

American children were not the only youngsters whose intensive television habits have been studied. Major descriptive studies on the subject have been conducted in several other countries, including those of Great Britain's Himmelweit, Oppenheim, and Vince; West Germany's Maletzke; Russia's Glushkova; Hungary's Schüller, Devai, and Kodar; and Japan's Takeshima, Tada, Fujioka, Kikuchi, Muramatsu, and Hamoda.

Sixteen years ago Himmelweit and her associates completed a three-year interview and survey study of 1,834 pairs of British children. At that time, the control partners did not have television reception in their town. The research group also did a pre-TV/post-TV study with 370 cases in a town which received television for the first time during the course of the investigation. While researchers reported that the evident heavy televiewing displaced leisure and study time, they concluded that television was neither a help nor a hindrance. Remarkably, the same researchers also reported that younger and slower youngsters each gained a four- and five-month advantage on knowledge over children without television (p. 406).

The study conducted by Glushkova in 1970 was sponsored by the Russian Institute of Health. From the findings, the researcher concluded that heavily watched television was a totally negative experience and, noting an apparent need for limiting this popular activity, recommended that children should watch television no more than thirty minutes per day. On a more promising note, the Hungarian researchers, Schüller and associates, by means of home surveys, found that heavy televiewing appeared to extend a child's horizons and areas of interest.

The investigation by Takeshima and his colleagues, conducted in Japan and reported in 1971, was almost a duplication of a major one carried out twelve years earlier by another Japanese researcher, Furu. The original study was a large-scale survey in Shizuoka over a two-year period in order to determine the influence of highly popular television on children. The present study was carried out using the same techniques. Some specific topics of interest were TV program preference, televiewing attitudes, and parental control over televiewing. The study sampled over 8,000 persons, including 1,444 third graders, 1,121 fifth graders, 1,378 junior high students, 1,319 mothers of children in kindergarten, along with 3,355 other mothers.

These investigators declared that the findings of this immense study revealed most children to be heavy televiewers, and that these youngsters preferred, as shown in most other countries' findings, action drama, family-situation drama and comedy, and cartoons (p. 17). It also demonstrated that Japanese preschool children were extremely interested in television to the extent that they watched it from two to four hours a day. Surveys indicated that "ninety-four per cent copied the words used in the program, 81 percent imitated something learned from programs in play, and 76 percent copied actions and styles which appeared on programs" (pp. 29-31).

SURVEY OF TV KNOWLEDGE/INTEREST

If both the regularity of my own observations and the magnitude of the worldwide studies fail to convince you that we need consider commercial television among formidable childhood interests, I suggest that you conduct some such research of your own, first with adults (who are generally first-generation TV viewers) and then with children, a second and "always" generation, having had television all their lives. This is the way I went about it, at the same time confirming what my earlier guessing and the large research projects had already suggested.

1. I first brought up the subject of commercial television with adults. As long as I didn't mention children (at which point adults will tell you what they have heard and read about the negative effects of television), I found that adults are about as enamored of TV as their children are. I listened with surprise to the astonishing quantity of details the adults enthusiastically related about popular programs, particularly when sharing the humor of some situation recently viewed.

My most interesting observation was among well-educated men, who claimed little or negative interest in commercial television, as is vogue. However, it did cause me to consider that when the podium guest remarked that "He could not believe he ate the whole thing," these men laughed. Now why, I mulled, would these anti-commercial television men laugh at the use of a television commercial in a university speech, if, in fact, they were not familiar with that commercial in its original setting in prime time?

2. I decided to check on the commonality of television with elementary children. I brought up the subject and was able to establish instant and gleeful rapport, to captivate large group attention for long periods, and to elicit high, high motivation! All I had done was ask children to tell me about commercial television.

THINKING GAME EXPERIENCE

I then asked each schoolchild (the same could be done with our own children) to tell me the name of his or her favorite show. I listed all the shows named on the board for every child to see. We then played THINKING GAME, an experience in which a child secretly selected one of the television program titles and offered the rest of us eager listeners a clue to the setting, plot, or characters of that program. I was astounded by the stored knowledge which the children possessed about television programs as shown by their incredibly detailed guessing, explanations, and clues. I was also able to reconfirm the years of noticing that when TV is the topic, ALL the children pay close attention AND eventually try to participate because each can. The outpouring and urgency with which every child contributed was hard to believe. The time passed with great speed, and the children complained that too soon they were required to stop for lunch.

Every time I tried this technique thereafter it became and becomes clearer that commercial television is a source of interest and information for most children. I began to develop other ways to extend THINKING GAME experience (see chapter 4).

SUMMARY AND CHALLENGE

And so it is for the reason that researchers such as Himmelweit et al., Witty and Kinsella, and Murphy and Gross are telling us that children are choosing to invest as much as a third of their waking day televiewing, that we need to find out how such a common and constant experience can be channeled to benefit children. Feeley has written that it is "therefore television, more than any other medium, that furnishes a common body of information for the early socialization of children" (p. 141). I might say that I have given you in this chapter, in the words of Gattegno, "a call to use television for what it can give, which is really tremendous and by most still unsuspected" (p. 4).

In the past, teachers and parents have tried to capitalize on children's interests both in school and at home. We have shown colorful, fanciful movies in class, and we parents have asked Mickey Mouse to help children tell time. If home TV is so interesting to our youngsters, surely there are some ways this TV experience can be used or channeled to help children.

This chapter gave you some primary reasons to explore TV use. In the next chapter I will review the growing variety of general comments and studies seeking and suggesting positive, specific ways to use television to help children learn.

Beginning here I have also left some room for your own thoughts on this whole subject of TV use. You will find similar spaces provided at the end of each chapter, in a dozen places within chapter 4, and at the end of the Bibliography.

My Own TV Notes:

Pioneering Positive TV Use

TEACHERS' USE OF TV

Despite the widespread interest in the educational potential of public television's "Sesame Street" as reported by Ball and Bogatz and despite the accumulated reports of studies showing the vastness and constancy of commercial television's child audience, few teachers have used commercial television at school. By this I do not mean to suggest that commercial telecasts be seen in class. I mean that teachers have rarely made use of commercial television in any manner. They haven't yet considered commercial television as a motivating, experiential background for academic study. And, of course, this book has been written to help us consider just that.

For example, in the primary grades, where teachers might introduce initial consonant sounds associated with the names of popular television characters, I have yet to find a teacher who does so before I suggest it. And in high school, where reluctant readers may not be easily induced to scrutinize **The Three Musketeers** by Dumas or even more modern material, it is unlikely that most English teachers have introduced the "Mod Squad" program as an attention-grabber for discussion with obvious parallels. There are, however, some high school teachers who are using television, as you will learn later. More commonly, an educator's use of home televiewing experience has been limited so far to an infrequent special program which he both selects and assigns. Such shows are previewed for teacher preplanning in periodicals such as **Teachers' Guides to Television** and in **TV Guide**. But use of the most popular student-selected programs has remained practically nonexistent. During an informal survey in 1971 of forty colleagues in two schools, I found that no teacher was familiar with even the name of "Prince Planet," the commercial television program at that time most-watched by children in their school.

We teachers have had, of course, very good reasons for not incorporating commercial television data in classroom experience. Teachers are always functioning under the pressures of time, of numbers (in students), and the expectation that we "cover" enormous amounts of required material. It is ironic that disciplinary problems usurp so much teacher time, problems which have often been linked to lack of relevancy in the experiences both teachers and students undergo.

It may also be that not using commercial television data is linked to the generally negative attitude held about it. Citizens' concerns about advertising exploitation and governmental studies such as the one edited by Rubinstein, Comstock, and Murray about violence and other effects have probably established unconscious avoidance of commercial television among learning alternatives. For example, in December of 1973, on an outstanding morning talk program, an eminent panel of experts was interviewed concerning children and television. Although this discussion continued every morning for a week, I heard few, if any, suggestions that we could or should use television **as it is** for any worthwhile purpose.

Therefore no one is to be blamed for not seizing the opportunity to use commercial television. Fourteen years have passed since television researchers Witty and Kinsella stated that "there are untapped possibilities for utilizing the interest engendered by television to further constructive individual and group endeavor" (p. 802). In 1966 Murphy and Gross stated that "educators are still far from grasping the real nature and potential of television" (p. 10). Although we teachers still do not commonly promote commercial television use, there are definite signs, as you will see described below, that we are beginning to tune-in to the idea.

To be fair, a few teachers and others are currently trying learning techniques derived from commercial television data and motivation. While difficult to locate, reports of such learning experiences are appearing more frequently in educational journals. Most of these positive statements were informal reports which, while enthusiastic, lacked the documentation of more rigorous experimental design. The group selected below do, however, deserve recognition as pioneers in this new field.

SELECTED POSITIVE PIONEERS

Folger, 1953, suggested that students would benefit from studying television as a medium.

Blakely, 1954, offered at least a dozen suggestions for the use of television stressing involvement and knowledge and a hope for a relationship between commercial television stations and educational institutions. He stated that "the educational possibilities of the media of mass communications have only been scratched" (p. 273).

Spiegler, 1956, reported he had made successful book selections for boys based on observable television interests in children.

Postman, 1961, detailed the comprehensive use of television in the teaching of English, showing how it might be used both as an aid to other studies and as a subject of study. This is a valuable paperback.

Mason, 1965, reviewed the results of a study conducted at Florida State University in which 345 kindergarten to seventh graders were tested to determine the extent to which they learned words presented with printed stimuli such as Coca Cola drawn from television shows. The investigator acknowledged children could read the stimulus words, but made some errors such as calling Coca Cola "coke." He interpreted the results to mean that such word learning was not better for poor readers. He concluded that the study suggested ways of using televiewing habits of children to design reading instruction.

Van Allen & Allen, 1966, applied language experience to the study and use of television with a reading program for young children. They suggested the TV story box and making books about children's television preferences.

Witty, 1967, suggested that a program based on inherent interest in televiewing be used to enhance learning, thus ensuring wider use of the medium itself.

Rodgers, 1968, declared that television programs watched at home are a good environment in which children may recognize and apply language arts skills taught in school.

Gattegno, 1969, proposed that the instantaneous visual learning afforded by commercial television has valuable implications for education in an increasingly visually oriented society. In 1970 produced one-minute, phonetic word-building experiences in animated form, sandwiching them between commercial television programs on Saturday mornings.

Stumphauzer & Bishop, 1969, reported the successful use of an on-off switch in the presentation and withdrawal of television cartoons as reward or punishment in the elimination of thumb-sucking behavior.

Nylin, 1970, stated that educators need to know the definite "limitations and potential of such technology as commercial television" (p. 139).

Popham, 1970, constructed criterion-referenced test books of school attitude and self-concept using commercial television as one setting. For example, he asked students how they play the role that Batman plays.

Haney, 1971, suggested that commercial television could be effectively used in reading and discrimination learning.

Xerox Education Group, 1971, reported high interest among children asked to read oversized selected children's books from televisionlike screens in a literature program called Xedia.

Blair, Toole, & Laws, 1971, (with King Features Syndicate) noted the long-standing popularity of the film and recently TV character Popeye and used this comic hero as a learning motivator in career education comic books currently in use in many schools.

Ward, Reale, & Levinson, 1971, noted that children had an extensive knowledge of commercials and program titles.

Hatchett, 1971, reported comprehension based on television discrimination.

Hook, 1972, according to Mersand (p. 3) listed sixteen ways that both radio and television can be used to foster English comprehension.

Fasick, 1970, 1973, indicated, with some reservations, that language learning may accompany television viewing.

Becker, 1973, authored one of the first **positive** collections of practical reading activities derived from commercial television experience! In addition, the ideas included have already met with success in classrooms. The influence of this small booklet may be widely noted as its publisher is the prestigious International Reading Association.

Hipple, 1973, according to Mersand (p. 4) posed TV ideas for high school English classes which foster both the study of the medium and other English objectives.

Mersand, 1973, presented extensive reasons for using television. He stated that "although television as a means of communication is the newest of the arts, it has already stimulated many significant studies which English teachers can hardly omit if they wish to accomplish their main objectives" (pp. 1-2). He presented an outline for a four-year high school study of television as part of the English curriculum.

Savage, 1973, declared that teachers can use commercial television data in reading instruction. He stated that "the trick for the teachers is to get their pupils reacting to what they see and hear on TV" (p. 135). He also suggested fact-fantasy discrimination, speaking and writing topics, reviewing and producing, plot analyzing, comparative book and newspaper studies, and commercials as appropriate possibilities for using commercial television.

Breslin & Marino, 1974, declared emphatically that television unquestionably is such a staple item that children are in need of guidance in developing a critical literacy regarding it and accordingly suggested that children be helped to scrutinize and assess plots and commercials and to analyze the outcomes presented through their much-chosen medium.

Kaye, 1974, authored, as a cofounder of ACT (Action for Children's Television), an important information action guide for family use. She told us how we could become involved and suggested some steps toward TV literacy. You will want to see the "Children's Workbook" in Kaye's chapter 8, in which are presented several fine ideas such as TV diary and log which could help a child evaluate his televiewing.

Mills, 1975, stated that we must view TV as serious and significant and use TV homeviewing experiences to foster school learning. She organized and directed PTST (Prime Time School Television), a Chicago firm which provides information on the classroom use of evening prime time programs.

SUMMARY AND CHALLENGE

These creative pioneering efforts in TV usage obviously demonstrate the growing realization that commercial television, even in its present state, must be counted as a regular experience of immeasurable interest to most youngsters, and as such could be used to these students' advantages. They suggest that we capitalize on commercial television in the schools, just as music teachers have long since incorporated stage and movie music such as Walt Disney's "Mary Poppins" score in the regular music curriculum. To do this will take both acceptance of the TV use notion and some preparation, just as do all well-thought-out educational ideas.

It would be strange to think that we did not notice how commercial publishers have risked millions on the whole notion of using commercial television. We need only glance at any dime and drugstore coloring-book shelf or at the photograph shown below, to see many examples of paper dolls, stickers, activity books, and games and toys with animated and human TV celebrities or TV programs as the baiting theme. And it would be ironic if we actually ignore the fact that the Children's Television Workshop, which produces for public television both "Sesame Street" and "The Electric Company," is incorporating elements of Superman and Spiderman, fantastically popular **commercial** television heroes, in their latest productions!

Yes, it certainly appears to make sense that we use commercial television in learning, that is, if the reported growing interest actually justifies this idea. Therefore, in the next chapter I will describe four recent large-scale research projects specifically designed to find out the effectiveness with children of reading and thinking techniques derived from television. These frontier educational studies, all conducted in the early seventies, give us more independent and significant reasons to try TV at school.

My Own TV Notes:

Four Frontier
T V Channels !

 In the spring of 1972 I conducted my own investigation to determine the positive learning potential of commercial television, the first experimental study specifically designed to do this with first-grade children. The major purpose of this research was to find out if multiple-choice questions derived from daily watched commercial television shows could, if presented as a pictorial experience, affect the thinking of first-grade boys. Only boys were included because I was also considering the academic and behavioral problems often characterizing boys.

This study was conducted at Arcola Lake Elementary in Dade County (Miami), Florida, a primary school. The 106 English-speaking boys who participated in the study were located in four pods, the equivalent of eight first-grade classrooms.

I met with every boy for three individual interviews over a month's time. At the first interview the experimental boy was asked to describe six commercial television programs previously determined as most-frequently watched by boys. The shows were "Gomer Pyle," "Gilligan's Island," "Flipper," "Popeye Playhouse," "Flintstones," and "Prince Planet." Each experimental boy was then asked to respond to four higher-order questions about the same programs that demanded more than knowledge of facts. During the second interview, each experimental boy responded to the special HITONTV (HIT ON TV) experience, a series of fifty-five cartoon-pictorial questions based on the same programs and designed for my study (p. 124-154). "HIT" in the title of the experience is an acronym for How I Think. An example of one question asked is:

"If you dropped a camera off a bridge, show me who could help you best."

The students then pointed to one of the five picture "answers," including cartoon likenesses of Gomer Pyle, Gilligan, Popeye, Flipper, and Fred Flintstone. Most boys picked Flipper. Other examples of questions asked are included on pages 17 and 61.

The control boys simply talked about the same six television programs during both of their first two meetings. During the final interview, all boys were administered the Ammons' Quick Test, a pictorial criterion measure of verbal comprehension. The results of the statistical tests indicated highly significant differences between the experimental and control groups in verbal comprehension. These findings seemed to indicate that the experimental boys benefited from their experience with higher-order questioning drawn from their favorite commercial television programs. I found that all the boys in the study seemed happy with the TV experience. The experimental boys could actually answer the fifty-five difficult questions. The only problem with the study was that the girls were unhappy that they were excluded!

In this chapter I have included a detailed look at three other frontier studies of commercial television use. These projects were also attempts to find out if a commercial television learning technique actually worked. The studies were devised independently from one another, which makes their overwhelmingly positive results, and in one case, its experimental significance, more important to the whole positive TV premise. All these large projects tell us we can utilize the medium, and the investigations notably relate to us different things we might try, different experiences to channel television data and interest.

PHILADELPHIA/DUAL AUDIO TELEVISION—BORTON

In 1971 Borton reported the first findings of what became the largest experimental research study to date examining the use of commercial television. This researcher, having arrived at the notion

A. Beating Brutus is like saving _____ (#3)
1. Wimpy   2. Flipper   3. Olive Oyl   4. Fred Flintstone   5. Gomer

Popeye characters (c) King Features Syndicate 1975
Flipper   Ivan Tors Films, Inc.
Fred Flintstone   Hanna-Barbera Enterprises, Inc.
Gomer Pyle   Ashland Productions

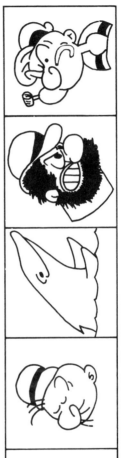

B. The person who would really like to eat at McDonald's is _____ (#2)
1. Fred Flintstone   2. Wimpy   3. Flipper   4. Brutus   5. Popeye

of potential use already outlined in this book, investigated the idea that children can learn factual information, concepts, and cognitive process skills while watching commercial television. Borton contended that children cannot by themselves effectively process the mass of television information they receive. He proposed an intervention procedure, "dual audio television," which is the addition of an FM audio track to which the child listens while viewing a regular commercial television program. Borton had a dual radio announcer speak to the watching child during the nondialogue spaces. The announcer tried to help the child relate to what he viewed and to understand it. For example, in a report of one of his studies in 1972, Borton used a highly watched afternoon program, super-hero, fantasy-animated "Astroboy." After the telecasts and dual audio listening experience, the participating children showed greater comprehension of what they had seen than did children who watched without Borton's procedure.

Recently, in an article by the Associated Press (1975b), Borton announced similar success with specific vocabulary building by employing his dual audio procedure using "The Flintstones" with Philadelphia children aged six to eleven. Borton also discussed potential use of his procedure on a national scale.

PHILADELPHIA AGAIN/TV SCRIPTS
SOLOMON AND McANDREW

Waters reported that Solomon and McAndrew, two school teachers from Philadelphia, made very positive use of commercial television. These teachers rescued extremely reluctant readers by using television scripting. As classroom researchers, the teachers taped popular television programs and reconstructed the scripts of the shows. They then invited children to read the scripts while watching the shows. The interest and success of the children was immediate! So promising was this technique with the junior high students that the teachers sought and acquired the use of actual scripts and film clips from the programs from excited show producers. In 1973 scripts were drawn from "Sanford and Son," "Kung Fu," "The Waltons," "Here's Lucy," and "Mod Squad" and used with the result that students read many scripts with gusto and glee. The students learned from the directions of the camera operator. Teachers remarked on the enthusiasm and reading accomplishments of students. Self-discipline and relevancy appeared linked together in the teachers' joyous evaluation of this technique for motivating low-achievers. Teachers pointed out the possibilities for learning word analysis, creative expression, and even typewriting in this television use.

Interestingly, the technique which Solomon and McAndrew have pioneered is inexpensive.

NEW JERSEY/TV TIE-IN BOOKS—HAMILTON

In a 1974 article entitled "TV: A Promising Tool for Teaching Reading," the editors of **Education U.S.A.** reported the work of Hamilton at Jersey City State College. Hamilton's study, related to reading instruction and commercial television, considered the reading habits of 350 junior high school students. This researcher discovered that these students were reading "three times as many tie-in books as customary titles" (p. 97). Tie-ins are books which are derived from movies or popular television programs, such as **Cool Cos** by Cohen, a biographical story about Bill Cosby, creator of the animated Saturday cartoon, "The Cosby Kids."

The editors of **Education U.S.A.** also reported Hamilton's finding that reluctant readers attempted tie-in books eagerly because of their intense interest in films and television. In addition, the editors related Hamilton's contention that such interest can create in students such a reading habit that the possibility of their later enjoyment of fine literature is improved. In **Instructor** magazine, Hamilton recommended that we offset TV's ills by helping children use it wisely, employing their "interest to motivate effective reading and learning" (p. 68).

SUMMARY AND CHALLENGE

And so it now can be said that professional interest in the positive use of commercial television not only exists, but exhibits every degree of commitment from conjecture to controlled experimental research study. If we believe that this recent focus on the idea constitutes reason to use commercial television, we need only begin to decide what we will do with it. For tomorrow is none too soon to begin to reap some of the benefits for children that we have read about.

The next chapter includes a collection of specific TV-related experiences logically derived from commercial television data and interest. It opens with eight suggestions that will help you use the chapter effectively. The experiences in chapter 4 are designed to assist your own use of TV—to help children learn.

My Own TV Notes:

Many Other Channels

HOW TO USE CHAPTER FOUR

"We interrupt this book for the following special report" would be a good way to start this chapter, because this chapter is long and filled with practical ideas, making it the picture tube of this book. What you will find on the pages that follow are numerous classroom-tested learning experiences which are derived from commercial television material. I am calling these applied TV ideas experiences, because I believe that each idea is an alternative exposure or experience in a skill or content area. Listed below are important organizational points unique to this chapter which will help you to use it effectively.

1. Look in the Index under "Experiences, kinds," in order to determine what experiences are included and to select the ones which best suit your students' needs. You will find many types of reading and thinking skills, math, science, social studies, and career education experiences included.

2. The arrangement of the chapter is by experience title. Many titles reflect the TV experience suggested. Browsing will give you

some ideas, but you may also wish to look in the Index under "Experiences, titles."

3. Primary, intermediate, and secondary experiences are included in the chapter as shown in the level headings next to the right margin. I have included the junior high school level within both intermediate and secondary experiences. Since most TV ideas are adaptable to older or younger children, the headings really indicate at what level the particular experience took place. As a teacher, you should look at all experiences, keeping in mind that you can easily adapt most experiences to other levels. Though a few experiences are not suitable for younger children, some unexpected ones are labeled "primary" because TV data elicited thinking from them not normally expected until the later grades.

4. You will notice that particular TV programs mentioned are no longer being shown, or you may think of other appropriate and currently popular shows not included. The experiences suggested here do not depend for their success on the specific data from any particular program. With a single watching, by reading in a TV reference such as **TV Guide**, or by asking students, you will be able to supply new or better TV data for experiences with ease. The experiences in this chapter are to serve as stimulating models.

5. The decorative rule, *******, indicates that the next paragraph is another version of the same experience, perhaps at a different level.

6. The last experience in this chapter, page 104, is entitled WOULD-LIKE-TO-TRIES. This experience consists of several blank pages on which you can make notes about adaptation, record anecdotes about use, or write out brand new ideas to try.

7. I have found that the first experience you should try is THINKING GAME, discussed first in chapter 1, page 6, and in more extensive detail in this chapter on pages 77-79. This is an exploratory TV experience that both children and teachers have enjoyed.

8. At some point I suggest you be sure to try USE TRANSFER (see pages 86-88). This experience helps children become conscious of ways they can use TV for learning.

My Own TV Notes:

LEARNING EXPERIENCES USING TV

ALPHA ORDER	Primary
Experience: Placement of words in alphabetical order	Adapts to all ages

We all agree that one skill we must learn is how to alphabetize. There are many ways to encourage students to learn this skill, but most of the time we ask them to alphabetize lists of words in which they have little interest. It is usually a long time before primary students begin to see the need for alphabetizing. I suggest that you try ALPHA ORDER, an early experience in using alphabetical clues. Here is what we did:

I first asked children to name their favorite programs, telling them I would make a book listing their programs. This would be a book for them to read, discuss, and illustrate. I asked them how we could remember where each program was listed in the large, looseleaf book we would make. We listened to all the suggestions offered and acted out, using a few examples, the possibilities and difficulties of numbering and random entering.

I then suggested that the children examine the idea that the programs be listed by their first letters matched to the posted alphabet chart they already knew. Together we conducted an experiment using this idea. Every time a child thought of another program, I asked the class to decide in which letter column they thought the program's name should be entered. After a few days of ALPHA ORDER practice in this TV-related fashion, most of the class could help make accurate ALPHA ORDER decisions.

To give you an idea of how some of the letter lists looked, samples are listed below. Keep in mind that these lists were constructed by matching the initial letter of a word seen with a letter seen. In the next experience, we will describe making lists according to sounds.

A a	B b	D d
"Addams Family"	"Bugs Bunny"	"Devlin"
"Adventures of Gilligan"	"Bob Newhart"	"Doctors"
"Adam-12"	"Bewitched"	
"All in the Family"	"Born Free"	
"Apple's Way"		

Many Other Channels

E e	**F f**	**G g**
"Emergency Plus 4"	"Fat Albert"	"Get Smart"
	"Flintstones"	"Gunsmoke"
		"Gambit"
		"Good Times"
		"Getting By"

* * * * * * *

This experience could of course be adapted to a writing format. It also provides opportunity for extending ALPHA ORDER beyond the first letter experience in the account above. High interest in TV sparked special interest in ALPHA ORDER experience, and, of course, that's exactly what I had in mind.

B FOR BATMAN   Primary

Experience: Auditory recognition/   Adapts to all ages
            initial consonants

Examples of initial consonant sounds are often limited to ones we've long used such as "d is for duck" or "b is for ball." We have asked, "What word can you think of that begins with the same sound as baby?" An amazing response came from children when it was suggested that "d is for Devlin and Disney" and "b is for Batman and Burnett!" The students were eager to think of other examples they have **heard** so many times on television. One teacher I know, after first playing B FOR BATMAN aloud, added child-suggested TV examples to her alphabet-sound correspondence chart the rest of the year.

* * * * * * *

Another version of B FOR BATMAN is teacher use of TV titles and characters as examples for many other sound-matching activities. I found that consonant and vowel combinations could be explained easily with such TV examples as the following: (sp) as in "Speed Buggy"; (br) as in "Brady Bunch"; (pr) as in "Prince Planet"; and (oo) as in "The Rookies" and "Scooby-Doo." I suggest you try TV sources for phonetic examples to meet your students' particular needs. You will also want to look at the experience VOWEL WOW, described on pages 92-93 of this book.

* * * * * * *

Still another version of B FOR BATMAN is the experience of hunting other word analysis examples among the array of TV titles and characters. I liked the following examples discovered and compiled by children:

compound words	plurals	contractions
"Manhunter"	"Valley of the	"That's My Mama"
"Flintstones"	Dinosaurs"	"Let's Make a Deal"
"Ironside"	"Superfriends"	
"Superfriends"	"Good Times"	

word shapes	little words in big words	syllabication
"Zoom"	"Born Free"	(identified title and number of syllables "clap-clap-clap-Scooby Doo")
"Hudson Brothers Razzle Dazzle Show"	"Little House on the Prairie"	"Scooby-Doo"
"Scooby-Doo"	"Mannix"	"Kung Fu"
	"The Waltons"	"Sanford and Son"
	"Six Million Dollar Man"	"To Tell the Truth"
		Samantha
		Redd Foxx

CAMERA PRETEND   Intermediate/Secondary

Experience: Selection of story   Adapts to older
            detail to fit
            author's purpose

I asked children to help decide what details we should include in a super-8 movie that would help create mood or plot movement. Although we were actually making a short film, this same experience is quite satisfactory when related to analyzing TV programs. For example, I asked students to imagine they were camera operators filming a chase scene in a segment of "Mannix." The students were encouraged to decide exactly where they would aim their lenses in order to create a mood of excitement, danger, and plot action. As you may imagine, the first responses were many, but superficial. Then they began to consider fine points which would help the viewer see and feel what the author intended. I was pleased at suggestions similar to "I would have to aim the camera at oncoming cars and stand on a moving vehicle so the audience would be almost as worried as Mannix. So they would think they were in his car!"

Other provocative examples for which students planned camera shots were

| "Creature Feature" | Young woman sits at desk unaware of monster slowly approaching behind her. |
| "The Lucy Show" | Lucy appears at her house in wet clothes and covered with mud just in time to meet important guests Ricky has brought home to dinner. |

Here are several other scenes which children have suggested for story detail analysis: the excitement of a parade; the sadness of a boy's dog dying; the tension of a girl winning a cross-country race; the fear of someone lost.

If you enjoy this viewpoint experience, you may want to try FILMMAKERS, an experience described on pages 35-36.

CAREER CATHODE   Intermediate/Secondary

Experience: Development of   Adapts to all ages
            awareness/television
            career

Television is of such high interest to most students, there is little wonder that I am often asked about TV jobs. While many young people are interested in television acting, I found that numerous others want to know about the technical aspects of television occupations. Accordingly, you might wish to include in your career education program experiences such as CAREER CATHODE by which students can obtain accurate information about how people in television work. One good way to find out is to ask television professionals to visit with small groups of youngsters for informal questioning and demonstrations. Some of the people who are informative guests include set designers, camera operators, choreographers, lighting specialists, makeup-people, directors, actors, producers, graphic artists, and news reporters, among hundreds of TV workers available. The nice thing is that in almost every area there are some of these professionals willing to volunteer an hour or so as a guest career specialist.

Before such a guest visits, you should help students compile a list of questions that they want answered. Such questions usually reflect great student interest in career training required, rewards, problems, and advancement opportunities. For CAREER CATHODE with a TV camera operator, one group of sixth graders compiled the following questions:

1. How does a camera operator achieve special effects such as enlargement (as in the Maxwell House coffee can); slow motion; stop-start (as in Purina Cat Chow-Chow-Chow); tricks (chuckwagon into wall); people flying, etc.?

2. How much time is actually spent in filming short commercials and also our favorite half-hour shows? How much time is spent editing?

3. Describe editing and splicing.

4. How would a camera operator on the street cover a parade or a chase episode with the police and a thief?

5. Of what value is the camera operator as a storyteller? (The students were thinking of close-ups, hidden evidence, secret clues, advance warnings, characterization, etc.)

6. How does being a TV camera operator differ from working as a camera operator for movies in Hollywood?

* * * * * * *

There is much to be learned from a visit to a television station. Students interested in CAREER CATHODE experience would find fascinating the terms and actions they could observe during an actual telecast. After such an observation they would enjoy talking with the people who made such a TV program possible. I will never forget how it felt to watch the "Munsters" and then to wander about the "Munsters" set examining and asking about incredible, rubbery cobwebs which gave the set realism. Knowing about television careers is to better appreciate the marvel that television really is, if used well by those who watch it.

CARTOON COMP   Intermediate

Experience: Analysis and interpretation   Adapts to older
            of cartoons

Many newspapers and Sunday comic sections often have regular TV-related jokes and cartoons. These pictorial remarks on TV can be a fine visual-print resource for work in comprehension. One way to provide such experience is CARTOON COMP, an event which many children have enjoyed. Reprinted here are two Channel Chuckles by Bil Keane as examples of cartoons that are particularly good sources for student interpretation. The questions below are typical of some I have used with these cartoons to foster comprehension.

"There, Igglenuk! THAT'S
what I'd like — a little
house on the prairie!"

Where does this joke take place?

What is happening inside the igloo? Explain how you know this.

Could this cartoon picture really happen?

Why did the artist plan the caption as coming from an igloo?

What would you have to know to write and/or understand this joke?

*   *   *   *   *   *   *

Of course another way to play CARTOON COMP is to display the cartoon with the actual caption covered. Invite the students to create their own captions based on the TV data they see in the cartoon. List and discuss the suggested captions. Eventually reveal the cartoonist's own caption as an additional tool for understanding the cartoon. Playing this version of CARTOON COMP helps students to understand what the creator of a cartoon was thinking and trying to express. Some children may initiate the additional experience of creating both cartoons and captions about television. A collection of these student cartoons would make excellent reading comprehension material for classmates and the substance of a fine letter to the TV cartoonist whose work originally stimulated the cartooning experience.

* * * * * * *

I placed a collection of TV cartoons taken from newspapers on five-by-eight-inch index cards. After writing and pasting-on five comprehension questions for each cartoon, I laminated the cards. These CARTOON COMP cards were one pleasant source of comprehension practice for the rest of that TV season.

* * * * * * *

Why is "Hairy O" a funny star to have on "Planet of the Apes?"
What language idea did the artist use to make this joke funny?
Could this joke be as funny if read aloud?
What would you have to know to create this cartoon?
Why would an artist select TV as a source for cartoons?

12-27-74   Bil Keane

". . . with this week's special guest star — Hairy O."

CLASS CHARACTER

Experience: Recognition of
class character traits

Adapts to older primary

Almost every day we hear about some group's concern with how they are characterized by the media. One way in which a critical concern about commercial television may be developed is to examine the apparent character traits of various ages, sexes, occupations, religions, and races as depicted on the television screen. Youngsters can be helped to recognize and argue the relative reality, accuracy, fairness, and purpose of different groups' TV "images." I have found older students fascinated with such a study in the experience I call CLASS CHARACTER.

Invite students to make a character-trait statement about one of the groups of people listed below. For example, ask them to describe TV doctors. In order to get a suggestion accepted, the student must offer an example from a well-known program such as "Marcus Welby" or "M*A*S*H*" which supports his characterization. Challenge the class to accept or deny the truth of the suggestions. The reality and fairness of the collective image of TV doctors should be explored. Students might be encouraged to interview real doctors to get the physicians' opinions of the TV doctors' traits. Students might select and read magazine articles on this same subject. One junior high class became angered at the way that they perceived young people are shown on TV; they wrote a critical letter to a network and to a producer of a program that they thought represented unfairly the way that most teen-agers really behave. Their reasoning was excellent in that they were concerned that many people believe the TV image of youth is true of all youngsters.

Here are other groups of people whose CLASS CHARACTER you will find provokes serious thinking in students:
What is the TV CLASS CHARACTER of:

women	men	married	single
teen-ager	child	divorced	widowed
boy	girl	bigot	friend
elderly	baby	tourist	enemy
bright	sick	rich	poor
disabled	slow	middle class	politician
blind	deaf	detective	police
drug abuser	insane	scientist	banker
criminal	alcoholic	homemaker	teacher

Many Other Channels

judge	law-abider	librarian	sponsor
black	white	entertainer	writer
Indian	Oriental	cowboy	athlete
Northerner	Southerner	minister	rabbi
Westerner	Easterner	priest	laborer
foreigner	farmer	industrialist	doctor
mother	father	reporter	technician
sister	brother	soldier	astronaut
grandparent	aunt	musician	poet
Protestant	uncle	secretary	scholar
Catholic	college	dropout	flight
Jew	student	lawyer	attendant

* * * * * * *

I also found it a natural extension of this experience to discuss the following questions with the students:

1. Once you have determined the way a group is portrayed, explain why TV projects such traits. Does it occur as a deliberate bias or for some other reason?
2. Is there any group we have examined whose CLASS CHARACTER traits might be considered positive by that group? If so, which group? Why do you think the group would like their TV image?
3. Which group, if any, do you think is represented most inaccurately?
4. Which group, if any, do you think seems most realistically portrayed on television? Is any negative trait given this group? If so, does this trait add or detract from reality?
5. If you were a member of a group depicted negatively, what would you do about it?
6. If you are a member of a group who believes they are accurately depicted, what, if any, action would you take?
7. Did you see any TV evidence that class descriptions are not always accurate for individual members of a group?

CONCLUDE   Intermediate

Experience: Conclusion from   Adapts to all ages
            story detail

I have used CONCLUDE in many ways. Students gain insight about the conclusion process by experiencing it. They draw logical conclusions about programs, characters, and personalities from descriptive detail given. For example, I offered students the following information about a TV star:

> Buddy Ebsen is a TV actor. He is an older man. He has been acting for many years. We have seen him on a commercial. We have seen him play both an unschooled but sensible mountaineer and a shrewd, homespun detective. From this paragraph you can CONCLUDE:
>
> 1. Buddy Ebsen always plays a backwoods person.
> 2. Buddy Ebsen can play several kinds of roles. (correct)
> 3. Uncle Jed and Barnaby Jones are not at all alike.
> 4. Television is the only place we have seen Buddy Ebsen perform.

Most students at first experience difficulty with CONCLUDE. They have not had many opportunities to untangle detail and restructure it into the logical relationships that CONCLUDE requires. So the answer or conclusion reached is not really as important at first as their responses to the question, "How did you come to that conclusion?" Their explanations of how they constructed a conclusion are essential because, by retracing their mental steps, the students may become more conscious of a process used in good thinking. Faulty reasoning can also be explored in informal CONCLUDE. I have seen students avoid earlier conclusion errors as a result of talking through CONCLUDE.

Be aware, of course, that CONCLUDE will likely require other specific thought processes. For instance, students who considered the information about Buddy Ebsen probably used synthesis in considering possible conclusion three. Students used comparison in item one, and it is likely that possible conclusion four required some analytic rereading and sequential thinking. CONCLUDE may be a frequent, brief experience, or the beginning of an elaborate study of comprehension processes. For some, this TV-related experience has proved a good introduction to conclusion skill.

My Own TV Notes:

When a child encounters an unknown word, one way that he or she may understand that word, of course, is to examine it in the context of the sentence in which it is used. Good readers count on swift use of this technique to enable them to understand what they are reading. Context may provide both the recognition and meaning of an unknown word. One way I have found to demonstrate to children how context operates as a reading cue is CONTEXT CUE. I used CONTEXT CUE based on TV data in three ways:

1. presenting a sentence with a missing word:
   Steve Austin easily threw the ball over ninety yards because his right _____ was really a machine.   (arm)

2. presenting a sentence with all words present, but one to be located which is inappropriate to the context:
   When the Addams Family arrived at the campgrounds with their terrifying animals, people, and sounds, all of the other campers became very happy. Soon the campground was deserted except for the Addams Family.   (happy)

3. Below are listed some words whose meanings I have extended by inviting children to associate them in the context of particular TV programs. See if your children can associate (match) the following words with programs in which they have particular meaning. Some may have two or more answers.

   1. **impossible** "Apple's Way," "Run, Joe, Run," "Kojak," "Six Million Dollar Man";

   2. **fierce** "Mission Impossible," "Superfriends," "Gilligan's Island," "Born Free";

   3. **disease** "Adam-12," "Columbo," "Marcus Welby," "Lucy";

   4. **officers** "Get Christy Love," "Scooby-Doo," "Lassie," "Hogan's Heroes";

   5. **league** "Bowling for Dollars," "Voyage to the Bottom of the Sea," "Karen";

   6. **overalls** "Jeffersons," "Sanford and Son," "Good Times";

7. **packing**	"Movin' On," "All in the Family," "The Waltons";
8. **members**	"Speed Racer," "The Waltons," "Bewitched," "Mickey Mouse Club";
9. **damage**	"Gilligan's Island," "Mannix," "The Three Stooges," "Barnaby Jones";
10. **apartment**	"Lucy," "Bewitched," "The Waltons," "The Odd Couple";
11. **balance**	"Six Million Dollar Man," "Tarzan," "Mary Tyler Moore Show";
12. **neighborhood**	"All in the Family," "Superfriends," "Jeffersons";
13. **dances**	"Mary Tyler Moore Show," "The Carol Burnett Show," "Sanford and Son."

COULD/COULDN'T

Primary

Experience: Determination of reality/fantasy

Adapts to all ages

This activity may be accomplished orally or presented to children in writing by asking them to indicate the statements that could not really happen. This requires, of course, that they also determine those statements that could happen. It is important that, whatever the choice, the children justify the answer given. An extension of the game might be to invite the youngsters to construct their own series of possible and impossible TV statements. Encourage them to try to stump their classmates. In my experience even small children become quite good at this activity. Here are some sample statements based on programs the children were watching in early 1975:

(C = COULD; CN'T = COULDN'T)

_____ 1. The six million dollar man ran after the truck and climbed up on it.

_____ 2. Right after Popeye ate the spinach, his arms grew very strong.

_____ 3. The lightning made Billy turn into Captain Marvel.

_____ 4. When the children were lost, they saw a dinosaur eating plants.

_____ 5. Grandma Walton rides on the back of the truck.

_____ 6. Scooby-Doo ate a sandwich as big as a house in one bite.

_____ 7. The speedy car talked to the children.
_____ 8. The Beverly Hillbillies found oil on their farm.
_____ 9. Joe saw the man and ran away barking loudly.
_____10. J.J. had a present for his mother.

It will be necessary that you tell the children that even if they have seen the event actually happen on the television program, they should decide if the event COULD/COULDN'T happen in real life. (Items 5, 8, 9, and 10 COULD happen.)

*　*　*　*　*　*　*

With older children you might ask if there is any relationship between the fantasy statements and the reason why particular programs are considered funny or popular.

FILMMAKERS	Intermediate
Experience: Production of a film	Adapts to all ages

Students love to make films. This experience is fun and a great stimulus for language arts skills. All you need is a super-8 camera and projector. Both can be rented, or your school system may have some equipment you can borrow. As filmmaking becomes more popular and the prices of equipment become more moderate, many teachers who make films with children are purchasing and enjoying their own equipment. I know at least one teacher who owns super-8 sound equipment and is having a wonderful time using it at school with her young filmmakers.

As for FILMMAKERS, a TV-related experience, this is how we went about it: I invited the students to decide what films to undertake, suggesting that they plan one fifty-foot reel about a familiar TV program and one reel on a special topic of student interest. The students chose to film their own version of "Kung Fu" and to depict how kites are made and flown. Another group filmed "The Six Million Dollar Man" and a student-written play about substance (drugs, tobacco, cleaners) abuse.

They finally shot six three-minute films which we then had spliced together and shown to the intermediate student body. Since these films were silent, I provided, as an accompaniment, a piano recording similar to those used with old silent movies. The student films were enthusiastically received, a just reward for all the work and learning that preceded the public performance.

During the filming of the TV short subjects, the FILMMAKERS discovered that hour-long TV programs do not condense well into three-minute shows. They also learned that such shortening creates a comic effect, and they eventually spent more time on fewer scenes. The students also grew in their appreciation of the difficulties encountered by a film crew on location. They were forever chasing curious onlookers off their outdoor "set" located behind the kindergarten.

Even if you do not have sound equipment, there is no reason why you cannot provide a taped sound track for films your students make. I do suggest that you settle for taping a student script based on comments students make while watching the finished picture. While I have not had much success with lip synchronization, I have had fine results with tapes of clever student commentary played simultaneously with the film.

* * * * * * *

You will have similar fun and high-interest application of language skills if you invite students to create snapshot exhibitions, slides, and filmstrips using TV ideas as story stimulators. The students become intrigued with visual production because the final result is very close in format and problems to what they have seen accomplished on television by professionals. Students who show particular interest in FILMMAKERS might also be encouraged to investigate career opportunities in this area, as in the CAREER CATHODE experience described on page 26. FILMMAKERS may also want to try the viewpoint experience CAMERA PRETEND described on pages 25-26.

FORMAT FACE   Primary/Intermediate

Experience: Preparation for   Adapts to all ages
              test formats

We know that we cannot expose children to actual test items before test day. We have the responsibility, however, to provide them with as much experience as is practical in testing. I do not mean to overdo testing but instead to make a conscious effort to expose children to test formats and test terminology they will be likely to encounter in actual testing. It is said that we must provide "test-wise" experience. FORMAT FACE is one way to do this in the attractive and captivating setting of familiar television. Some oral and written experiences using television content in a testing format provide children with a friendly orientation to sometimes difficult testing procedures and formats. See if you agree. The following sample "test-readiness" sheet suggests one way to use FORMAT FACE:

EXPERIENCE A

Directions to the teacher:

Place the questions on the board beforehand. Students might be encouraged to read the questions before listening to the paragraph in order to know what information they should listen for. Then read the paragraph aloud to the class.

Steve Austin, the "Six Million Dollar Man," is played by Lee Majors, an actor. On the program, Mr. Majors performs such tasks as jumping over high walls without a pole, seeing great distances without binoculars, and running at great speed without wheels. It is too bad for the thugs who steal something and try to escape from Mr. Majors on foot. They can never escape. Computers help Steve Austin. Cameras help Mr. Majors.

1. Mr. Majors can do unusual things because
   a. he has special body parts.   c. he plays Steve Austin.
   b. the camera makes it look   d. he is an actor.
      that way.
2. This story shows that Steve Austin does things that other people can do if
   a. they run very fast.   c. they have objects to help them.
   b. they help catch escaping people.   d. they spend six million dollars.
3. The word **played** in this story means
   a. had a good time.   c. teased.
   b. let out the line.   d. acted.
4. The **best** title for this story is
   a. Mr. Austin and Mr. Majors   c. Electronic Man Races
   b. Mr. Majors' Camera Tricks   d. The Money Man

* * * * * * *

During the same session, I provided students with EXPERIENCE B of FORMAT FACE, distributing a different paragraph about "The Three Stooges." This time, though, the material was for actual reading, and the children were "talked" through the answers. Since this paragraph was about a familiar and popular program, I was able to make the format the main objective of the experience.

GENERAL WORD SPY   Primary

Experience: Application of word analysis   Adapts to all ages
                 and vocabulary skills

Having a child or a class dictate their own material has long been a fine way to capture students' attention to the language arts. When the story dictated is about TV, I find that specific word attack and vocabulary skills can be applied extensively as a game. The story may be used just as written on the board or chart, or each child may have a copy of it. The teacher examines the material for its possibilities as a WORD SPY source, deciding what words are present in the children's story that are examples of particular decoding or comprehension skills presently being learned in that class or group or by that student. In the instance of WORD SPY shown in the "Spiderman" story on page 39, the teacher asked each child in the room to look carefully at the child-created story and:

1. Underline the word that begins with the same sound as **Spiderman.** (spins)
2. Put an X on the word that begins like **go.** (guy)
3. Underline the word that begins with the same sound as **jump.** (just)

4. Underline the word that rhymes with **hoots.** (boots)
5. Circle the color that begins like **run.** (red)
6. Put a squiggly line around the word that begins like **blow.**
(blue)

Spiderman

Spiderman has to fight the robbers!

By Robert

(Story dictation—child aged 7)

He spins a web
on a bad guy.
He can climb
up the sides
of buildings
just like a
spider. His boots
are red. His
pants are
blue. And his
back of his
shirt is blue.
His whole other body is red.

Some children came to the board and used chalk to indicate answers. Others, as in the example, indicated the answers on the copy of the story on their desk. The children checked the answers themselves. I believe that the same story could be used effectively in many other ways if the teacher decided that the children currently needed other specific skills. Some skills I thought of are vowel variants such as the er in spider; little words in big words (an, ant, pan, pant); inflectional endings like (s) in (spins); and other blends (climb, shirt).

Another exciting possibility is the use of this same story material for simultaneous vocabulary development. This same teacher asked the children to locate the words that meant:

1. an eight-legged animal. (spider)
2. places such as houses, offices, schools. (buildings)
3. three things to wear. (boots, pants, shirt)
4. makes something like a net from thread. (spins)
5. the opposite of front. (back)
6. the opposite of part. (whole)

One suggestion concerns duplication of children's stories for other children to read. The "Spiderman" story, as dictated to a school volunteer and used by her with the young author, was edited and typed with a primary typewriter before any other children used the story. A clear, well-lettered story will please the original author and serve as a visual model to other readers. Your editing, however, should not include rewording, but only corrections to written English such as capitalization and indentation expected of a teacher taking dictation. Hopefully, original dictation will be written down in good form in the first place.

My Own TV Notes:

HIGH-USE WORD SPY   Primary

Experience: Recognition basic   Adapts to all ages
            sight words

When discussing important reading concerns, almost every teacher will tell you that children do not readily learn the many small words which are used most often in English. Yet these are the words which hold the language together. Teachers have planned many ways that children might learn this basic sight vocabulary. We provide the children with flash cards and lists drawn from the famous Dolch or the more recent Kucera-Francis list noted by Johnson. You might try the following TV-related experience as still another way for children to learn the high-frequency words:

Present each of the children with a copy of a paragraph of a brief story one of the children has dictated to you about a popular TV program. Perhaps, as in the example "Planet of the Apes" on page 42, the story on the ditto might be illustrated by its young author. Ask the children to read the story silently as its author reads it aloud (with you, if necessary). Then ask the children to circle the high-frequency words that you dictate. After they have looked for the word on their own for a minute, say the word again and place it on the board or a chart where they can see it. Let them WORD SPY some more, perhaps with a friend as a classroom partner.

In my experience, the children enjoy reading a friend's dictated story about a television program. When youngsters are excited about the story, it is not difficult to encourage WORD SPY, a fine way to practice such sight words in other than a drill manner.

It is always good experience, as in HIGH-USE WORD SPY, to locate the sight words in a setting with meaning. In that way, the high use of such words is clearly shown and interest maintained. Children whose own stories are used for such spying of course show even greater interest in looking for words. One boy who had participated in the morning in HIGH-USE WORD SPY, "hunting" within some other child's story, came to the teacher after lunch with a sentence he had written about the program "Gilligan's Island." He wanted to know if the **teacher** could find the "words we always use" in the following sentence: "Gilligan and his friends were all on the island." Before the teacher could answer, he proudly told her the answers were "and," "his," "all," "on," and "the." He also added that he "had" to use the words to make sense. The teacher wisely used his sentence (with his permission) as an example for the whole class. He needed help to spell "Gilligan's" and "island" correctly, but he had learned the appearance and necessary use of some of the famous basic sight words.

This same teacher then asked the children to make up other clues. HIGH-USE WORD SPY is an elaborate but simple, exciting but serious way to apply skills. As with most TV-related activities, the children do not like to stop playing the good skill-builder WORD SPY.

BY Kenyon (Story dictation—child aged 7)

Planet of the Apes

Remember that astronaut was going up in the spaceship.
He fell down into the water.
The spaceman got out
He got caught in a net.
The planet of the apes had the net
and captured him. And they put him in a big cage.
After that a planet of the Ape Man went to the hideout.
He called the rest of the Planet of the ape soldiers. They had a big fight.

HUMOR US   Intermediate

Experience: Analysis of humor   Adapts older

We have all laughed. People who wish to make us laugh practice for years to achieve our chuckling admiration. Older students can learn much about humor by examining the various funny people who have long entertained us on TV. Students I know have observed TV comedy and comedians and gag-writers to try to determine why we laughed. Here are some TV data older students enjoyed evaluating:

jokes	ad-lib, timing, delivery, deadpan, second-take;
combos	The Three Stooges, Martin and Lewis, Abbott and Costello, Smothers Brothers;
writers	Carl Reiner, Johnny Carson's writers;
impressionists	Rich Little, David Frye;
roasts	people roasted, roasters;
slapstick	pratfalls, pies, sight gags, costumes, mistaken identity;
characters	cast of "Mary Tyler Moore Show," "All in the Family";
satire	David Frost, Carol Burnett;
sketches	"The Carol Burnett Show";
stars	Phyllis Diller, Lucille Ball, Jonathan Winters, Jerry Lewis, Milton Berle, the late Jack Benny;
dramatic "comedy"	"Baretta," "Columbo";
situation comedy	"All in the Family," "Jeffersons," "Sanford and Son."

I AM AUTHOR   Intermediate

Experience: Expression through   Adapts to all ages
             writing

We know many ways to stimulate youngsters to become authors. We have asked students at every grade level to dictate or to write stories. I AM AUTHOR is included as a novel alternative to encourage writing even among reluctant readers. One version of I AM AUTHOR was presented in the following way:

Each student was given a piece of twelve-by-eighteen-inch construction paper, each piece with a two-inch fold along the bottom of the long edge. The students were invited to draw a scene from each of their two favorite television programs in the spaces on the back and front upper sides of the paper.

While the students were drawing, I circulated among them and wrote below each person's drawing a dictated comment in the margin created by the fold. I encouraged able students to add their own descriptive sentences or conversation beneath the pictures. Each dictated sentence was begun with the student's name; for example, "Sam said, '. . . ,' " so that when the books were read aloud, each student would hear his or her name read also.

We stapled all the pages into three books similar to those shown below. In some classes, teachers laminated the pages. Everyone seemed to enjoy reading and hearing the books. Reluctant readers read and reread them. Some students read them to primary children. One room used I AM AUTHOR primarily as a writing project to help younger children read about television.

*   *   *   *   *   *   *

I AM AUTHOR may be highly individualized. The booklet included on page 45 is similar to those written by individual sixth graders. When pages like this in ditto form were folded, they each become a tiny volume, the individual author's pocketful of satisfaction. For most students I ran off only seven copies. Each author was given five, the perfect reward for himself and a gift for a few friends and his family.

*   *   *   *   *   *   *

You may want to try an exciting advanced version of I AM AUTHOR by encouraging students to write television scripts. This experience requires evaluation of program plotting, characterization, dialogue, and perhaps committee work and inquiry letters to television writers.

Creature Feature

I saw a TV monster.
It was scary and silly.
I was afraid. I was not
afraid.
I think I know how they did
the monster's makeup.
Did you see that show?

A TV BOOK

by Jerry Z.
Young Authors' Club

Two stories
March 7, 19XX

The Waltons

"The Waltons" is my favorite program. It is a good story but it is sometimes sad. The family is poor. The story takes place about forty years ago.

Richard Thomas is the star of the show. He plays John-Boy. This year John-Boy is going to college. But we still see him with the rest of his family back at home. I like the part at the end when everybody is talking just before they go to sleep.

In some instances, after very careful planning and writing, student-created scripts have been selected for actual presentation on the original television program. Students once wrote a script for "Bewitched" and had the great pleasure of seeing their work televised. Actual presentation, however, is not as likely a reward as the scriptwriting process itself. The students I know have greatly enjoyed the research and struggles connected with writing dialogue for their favorite TV characters and with plotting for the programs they most watch.

Further information about scriptwriting may be found in discussions and experiences with script**reading** on pages 66 and 96.

IDEA CENTER   Primary

Experience: Recognition of   Adapts to older
               main idea

We all need to realize the central ideas in what we read and hear. Commercial television programs can be used in many ways to stimulate student practice in determining main ideas. Though many variations will probably occur to you, here are two ways IDEA CENTER has proven successful:

I invited second graders to help decide the main idea of such programs as "The Waltons," "Superfriends," and "Chico and the Man," and listed all ideas suggested in simple sentences. Students were invited to eliminate or combine sentences with help until we had a single statement which the class agreed to be the main idea of the program.

Finding the main idea of a series was difficult for primary children. They found it far easier to analyze a particular episode. However, they enjoyed IDEA CENTER in both cases.

*   *   *   *   *   *   *

Some teachers have used IDEA CENTER by presenting TV-related paragraphs which must be matched to the correct main idea of four suggested. Here are two paragraphs used in this way.

> We saw "Superfriends" on TV. Aquaman cleaned up the oil spill from the boat. Batman helped pick up litter in a park. Wonder Woman was telling some men about the smoke from their factory. This story is about

a. being careful

c. "Superfriends," work on pollution. (correct)

b. the busy "Superfriends"

d. Pollution is bad for us.

On "Emergency" it had been three hours since an alarm bell rang. One fireman cleaned up the fire station kitchen. One man put together a model truck for his son. Two more firemen played chess. One was trying to figure out a wooden puzzle. Five firemen were upstairs asleep. Just then the fire bell sounded again.

The main thing this paragraph tells us is
a. Firemen play games.
b. We would like a firehouse.
c. Firemen are not always busy.
d. In between fires, firemen do many things. (correct)

* * * * * * *

Older children are interested in determining the main idea of documentaries and specials about world famine, teen-age alcoholism, political white papers, and fictionalized history. Older students also enjoyed IDEA CENTER as determination of the main idea of smaller story elements such as scenes and specific dialogue.

INTERVIEW   Intermediate

Experience: Experimentation with   Adapts to older
            interview procedures

Fifth-grade students enjoyed INTERVIEW. I watched several interview format TV programs with students, and we all took notes about particular procedures commonly used by interviewers. We also listed ways that particular interviewers differed. After watching Barbara Walters, David Susskind, and Bill Beutel, as well as local TV interviewers, we played INTERVIEW with various students as guests. One class found it had its own Johnny Carson. I laughed heartily as their interviewer talked with classmates who pretended to be famous personalities.

My Own TV Notes:

LETTERS

Experiences: Composition of
inquiry letters;
composition of fan
letters

Adapts to all ages

Few language activities connected with commercial television have created as much interest as TV LETTERS. This may be because the children involved have experienced a link among themselves, their favorite programs, and the real people who work in the television industry. Children are encouraged to ask for answers to their questions about television and to find out about how stars and technicians function. Children have written to:

stars	character actors	writers	producers
producers	local stations	FCC (Federal Communications Commission)	sponsors
camera operators	national networks	broadcasters	news people

I found that even the youngest children have many questions about programs which are best answered by television professionals. Some children dictated questions to be included in a group letter. Others wrote individual letters. The following letters are similar to those actually sent out by second and sixth graders:

to a star:	"I liked when you did that funny dance. But how did you change clothes so fast? You were messed up before. Can you send me a picture?"
to a camera operator:	"Can you please tell me how you get the little old wagon through the door?"
to a sponsor:	"I tried your cereal. It was not as good as you said, and the toy was not that big."
to a network:	"Why do you put all the good shows on at 8 in the night? My mother makes me go to bed at 7:30. Can you do something about it?"
to a local station:	"I enjoy many of the shows put on. But I am not happy about what you did now.

Why did you take 'Planet of the Apes' off? Everybody in my school watched it. Can you put it on again? We could not watch it before because of football games and practice Friday nights."

to a producer: "I really like 'The Waltons.' I wish I could meet Richard Thomas. I think he is nice. I hope the show goes on forever."

to a network: "I like scary monster shows. But I don't like when little children on TV almost get hurt. It makes me think of a boy in my city who got hurt."

I advise you to begin TV LETTERS as an early fall project if possible in order that children may still be with you for the experience of receiving a reply. It helps to speed the reply if you send a cover letter with the children's letters specifically requesting a prompt answer. Addressing envelopes and stamping them adds to the excitement of purposeful letter writing. Another tip is that you assure that the letter is actually mailed. I walked one class right to the mailbox. Here is a comment similar to one that was made that day en route to the mailing:

"I wrote a letter to Diahann Carroll. I saw her reading some on TV. I did not know where they came from. They came from another school I think. Maybe she will read mine on TV too."

LINGO   Intermediate

Experience: Translation of jargon   Adapts to all ages

Phrases and statements that we have been hearing on television for years are really not well understood by students. One good way to help youngsters better comprehend television is to play the experience LINGO.

I invited the students to listen to TV LINGO statements, explaining that I would like them to tell me what each statement meant. After each TV statement, I collected translations of what students believed had been said. Over a period of days I noticed improvement in interpretation. Where at first, some of the students said they had never "heard" any similar statements on TV, after a few days, many of them noted such statements on TV and reported back to me with far more mature thinking about what they had heard than at the beginning of LINGO experience.

Below is TV LINGO that I think you will recognize. I have provided these samples for your use in this experience, but I predict you will think of others.

"Before we sign-off . . ."
"Portions of the preceding were prerecorded."
"Sitting in for _____ will be _____ ."
"_____ , _____ , _____ will be with us."
"This program was filmed on location in _____ ."
"Portions of this program you may feel are too intense for preadolescent children or other persons who are watching."
"Portions of this program were filmed before a live audience."
"She will do fine in that time-slot. Look who she's opposite."
"We'll be right back."
"This program has been preempted by the following special. _____ , normally seen at this time, will return at its regularly scheduled time next week."
"We rejoin the network for the program already in progress."
"We interrupt this broadcast for the following special report."
"We regret that our video transmission is temporarily disrupted."
"The trouble is not with your receiver. We are experiencing video difficulty."
"At that time I was working for another network."
The anchorman misread the cue cards announcing, "And now a word from our sponsor. . . ." Actually he was supposed to say, "We'll break away now for a station identification."
"He was cancelled."
(You might imagine the wild guessing that first took place here.)

* * * * * * *

One anecdote about LINGO which I heard from a fifth grader was: "In that one where it talks about preadolescent, it means little children should not see it because it is too scary or you-know."

"You-know" (indicating recognition of sex as another censorable item) really means that youngsters develop some translation skills on their own. LINGO experience can only enhance their learning. Here are some more LINGO examples.

"The story that you have seen was true. Only the names were changed to protect the innocent."

"Any resemblance between these characters and any persons living or dead is purely coincidental."

"This editorial does not necessarily reflect the opinion of the station or the program's sponsor."

"That was the sketch that ended with a black-out."

*   *   *   *   *   *   *

Another version of TV LINGO would be to invite the students to suggest who might have said the various statements, considering what each statement means.

LISTEN-REMEMBER   Primary

Experiences: Recollection of details   Adapts to all ages
                 and sequence

LISTEN-REMEMBER is simply another way to capture children's attention to remembering details and sequence. Before a student can be expected to use these skills as he reads, he has to be able to use the skills in an auditory sense. Teachers have long been aware that precise listening is a language art which many students need to improve, and LISTEN-REMEMBER is a sure way to provide them with some productive listening experience. This concept has been used in the following ways:

Invite one student to tell the class the exact details of a program watched by many students the day before. Allow other students to inject details left out and events in the sequence that are omitted or in the wrong order. Make sure that all the students, and especially the one relating the program, understand that the purpose of the experience is to develop the most accurate retelling of details and sequence of events possible.

I found that this experience was enjoyed by everyone. I liked the fact that many youngsters could contribute, having seen the program, which, in the primary grade case we observed, was an episode of "Planet of the Apes." You will probably want to limit each LISTEN-REMEMBER to ten minutes per program so that another program can be retold. In this way most students will have the opportunity to contribute, having seen one or another of the programs.

*   *   *   *   *   *   *

Another version of LISTEN-REMEMBER is played this way: Invite the class to listen to you read something about TV. Explain that after you are through, you will ask them to repeat as much as possible of what they heard and in the order they heard it spoken. Once they understand what they are to listen for, read them a brief review of a new program, a few paragraphs from a TV book or magazine about a popular TV star or program, or a fictitious TV story. Attempt to create a brief story which has comprehension value in itself. Here is one I concocted for the LISTEN-REMEMBER experience.

> One of the funny things about the "Beverly Hillbillies" program is that the Clampetts never change. The family sees everything that happens from the point of view of uneducated mountain people. Being in Beverly Hills does not seem to make any difference. Here is an example of what we mean: Jethro has been living in the mansion for years and still thinks the swimming pool is a "cement pond." Uncle Jed is living in the middle of a rich neighborhood and still does not know that the neighbors hate his shooting his shotgun in the backyard. Grannie has not yet figured out that nobody can stand her cooking but her family. How can this be? Why don't the writers let the Clampetts learn?

After I read this selection, I asked the children to tell me what I was reading about. I invited as much detail from them as they could remember, and encouraged them to recall the sequence of description of family members. I asked them to tell me which family member was not mentioned. (Ellie Mae)

*   *   *   *   *   *   *

Of course, older children might answer the questions on paper or might play this experience as READ-REMEMBER. A super variation suggested by students is LISTEN-REMEMBER TEACHER. The class listens while a child tells **the teacher** about a program. The teacher is then asked to retell with the class listening for the inclusion of proper detail and sequence. This version of LISTEN-REMEMBER is a smash hit and learning experience for all involved.

MAP-DECIDE	Intermediate/Secondary
Experience: Inference/geographic location	Adapts to older primary

---

Some TV programs such as "Streets of San Francisco" and "N.Y.P.D." have as their setting a certain city. Even if the program is actually filmed on a studio set indoors and elsewhere, the TV director deliberately creates the impression that the action occurs in a specific geographic location. This location could be a city, a country, or region, but an impression of each place is developed by the inclusion in the filming of small details which you would expect to see in that location. As two characters are talking, for example, we see through the rear window of their taxi a view of the Empire State Building. We automatically infer that the action is taking place somewhere in New York City. Other details, such as a street sign that reads Broadway, subway entrances, and skyscrapers add to our impression. However, if we saw a palm tree growing next to one of the buildings, we might have some difficulty figuring out where the story is taking place.

The geographic location of a TV program is also often suggested by the verbal detail in the script. The skillful inclusion by the TV author of such remarks as "I saw it this afternoon near the Staten Island Ferry," gives students fertile audio material from which to infer location. You may wish to play the inferential experience called MAP DECIDE as follows:

A large world map should be placed so that it may remain a visual reminder and scene of activity for an extended period of time. Invite students to suggest where particular programs (less obviously located than the detective programs mentioned above) seem to take place. If a student can justify his decision on the basis of details he has heard or seen on the program to the satisfaction of his classmates, he may fill out a label with the program title and place it on the map in the appropriate spot. Should a program take place in two or more locations because of travel within the story or flashbacks, the student may also make those labels, provided again he can explain or justify those geographic locations.

I believe that students will be interested in continuing MAP-DECIDE. They may, as one group I know did, begin to recognize clusters of programs around certain locations on the map. Some regions and countries may also appear to be popular sites for television settings. Invite students to infer why this might be so. A discussion might ensue as to why TV people want to "fool" us geographically, anyway. Before they played MAP-DECIDE, I found that many children missed obvious weather, tree, and landmark clues. After I provided the experience, I saw a marked improvement in perception of geographic detail. I was able to elicit inference as to the importance of setting to author's purpose or plot line.

*   *   *   *   *   *   *

Two other variations of MAP-DECIDE, played similarly, would be TIME-DAY-DECIDE and MOOD-DECIDE. The main differences in these versions would be the charting of decisions. TIME-DAY could be charted on a giant clock face, and in MOOD-DECIDE students could construct a mood graph and plot the moods of programs they can both identify and support with program detail. For example, you could imagine the great contrasts that would be shown in TIME-DAY-DECIDE if a three-day investigation by Columbo was charted in sequence and next to it, the events of one evening of Scrooge in Dickens's **A Christmas Carol.** MOOD-DECIDE might prove quite interesting. Imagine the plotting with different colored markers of such programs as "Kojak," "Roadrunner," "The Waltons," and "Good Times." I think such experiences as TIME- and MOOD-DECIDE may produce materials which are good examples of time and mood in fiction as a characteristic of plot development and of characterization.

MEANING SHIFT   Intermediate/Secondary

Experience: Examination of multiple-   Adapts to older primary
                 shift words

Teachers are concerned that students at all levels become aware of the multiple meanings of many words in the English language. MEANING SHIFT is an alternative experience which promotes such an awareness. You might enjoy the experience in this way:

Invite the students to list with you as many words as everyone can recall which are related to television. Good sources for TV terms are the television guides and preview sections in newspapers and popular magazines. Another place to locate words is through listening to programs at home and listing special terms heard. Your list might look something like this:

channel	repeat	spin-off	set
tune	program	identification	tube
station	show	guest	vertical
cast	pilot	rerun	volume
special	antenna	network	cue
star	screen	feature	show

Since television terminology is generally adapted from the vast body of the English words already in use, it is likely that many TV terms are excellent examples of shifts in meaning—one of the shifts being, of course, use in the television industry.

Invite the students to give as many definitions as they can for each term. Encourage them to select from the definitions the one which could be called the TV meaning. Students might then use the terms in sentences, either in oral or in written form.

*   *   *   *   *   *   *

Younger children might best enjoy MEANING SHIFT if it were presented in oral form. They might also illustrate the various meanings of say, "show" with large colorful pictures. Used in this way, the experience can function as a readiness experience for shifts in meaning later seen in print.

*   *   *   *   *   *   *

Another variation of MEANING SHIFT would be to invite the students to experience it in opposite fashion. Ask them to design a new list of TV terms which they believe were coined for television and which seem to have no other meaning than the TV definition. Expect and encourage any challenges. Some words students suggested were sign-off, television, preempt, and studio. Depending on student experience, the students will select words such as these which they can easily verify or disqualify with dictionaries. Students who have tried MEANING SHIFT OPPOSITE declare that there are actually few, if any, words which are solely television words. Here we have the beginning of a study of word origins! What will your class decide?

MR. PREDICTOR
Intermediate

Experience: Prediction of outcomes
Adapts to all ages

MR. PREDICTOR can be used to improve skill in deciding likely outcomes. Actually, this process is used commonly and without much conscious effort. For example, we move the lamp cord to prevent an accident, hesitate to relate bad news, watch someone open a long-hoped-for present, or observe another person's right-turn signal. For each observation we promptly select a probable outcome based on both the details we see plus our knowledge of similar past events. Familiar content provides many opportunities for the conscious application of predictive skill.

Using the examples given below, I asked students to choose a logical outcome. I then invited them to explain their choices as well as to justify the elimination of other choices. I found that faulty prediction became the subject of humorous and interesting discussion.

1. "The Six Million Dollar Man" ran across the field at sixty miles per hour. He was running after an escaping animal. After a few minutes, this TV character
   a. became tired.
   b. was able to escape.
   c. captured the creature. (correct)
   d. won the race.
   e. called the police.

2. Brutus arrived at Olive Oyl's house. He saw an empty can. It was a spinach can. Brutus was not happy because he saw the can. Brutus was thinking that
   a. Olive Oyl ate dinner before he came.
   b. Popeye was ready for him. (correct)
   c. he was hungry.
   d. he did not like spinach.
   e. Olive Oyl was having spinach for supper.

3. Kung Fu was captured by two outlaws. He asked them for some water to drink. One of the outlaws went to the spring to get the water. That was a mistake for the outlaws because then
   a. the outlaw came back.
   b. Kung Fu was really not thirsty.
   c. the other outlaw was thirsty.
   d. Kung Fu was able to get away. (correct)
   e. the sheriff arrived just in time.

I realize that the students were in command of previous knowledge about the behavior of the TV characters used in the examples. However, in working through these examples aloud, I found that through this previous knowledge the students began to realize what prediction is and what it requires. I then played MR. PREDICTOR with the facts and previous experiences included in or suggested by the materials presented. For example, if no one had ever seen Popeye, I would have had to explain what happens to Brutus when Popeye eats spinach. Since students had seen Popeye in action many times, I found that they were able to make accurate inferential forecasts or predictions of outcome.

* * * * * * *

I know teachers who extended MR. PREDICTOR to TV news, weather, and sports forecasting. When MR. PREDICTOR was used

Many Other Channels

first, they found that students were able to make more appropriate decisions about future events, as they said, "based on the vibes" from present facts and past experience.

$$* \quad * \quad * \quad * \quad * \quad * \quad *$$

NOUN-VERB MATCH

Intermediate

Experience: Relation of noun to verb

Adapts to all ages

Teachers often look for ways to help children see relationships between the action and the one who acts. Several teachers have enjoyed NOUN-VERB MATCH to develop awareness of the noun-verb relationship, although the format of this experience may be adapted to many other language skills. One teacher provided NOUN-VERB MATCH in this way:

Fifth-grade students were asked to cut out all the words or phrases below, match the nouns with an appropriate verb, and paste the matched combinations on the sheet.

John-Boy	crashes	motorcycle	Christy Love
Scooby-Doo	Kung Fu	won	writes
is running	J.J.	solves	laughs

Students expressed great interest in this experience and worked together to complete it, amused by the match-ups of familiar TV personalities and likely actions. (They thought the cut and paste format was fun. It had been a long time since they pasted academic work.)

PICTURE SORT

Primary

Experience: Classification of pictures

Adapts to all ages

Pictures cut from TV magazines and from newspaper stories about programs can easily be used in PICTURE SORT, a classifying experience. Depending on the level of the children, students can be asked to sort, for example, twelve pictures into three groups of related pictures. Of course you can design this game to be as difficult as you wish, but in my experience, the first time it is played, you might wish to make the categories fairly obvious and, in fact, known. Below are several categories which teachers have used to TV PICTURE SORT. However, you might also wish to ask children to derive their own category headings. This procedure works well too, particularly in small groups.

sons	detectives	like to eat	workers
J.J.	"Hong Kong	"Cannon"	"Marcus Welby"
Clifton	Phooey"	"Scooby-Doo"	"Movin' On"
Donny Osmond	"Inch-High	"Fat Albert"	"Emergency"
	Private Eye"		
	"Sherlock		
	Holmes"		

Having placed the four categories on the board, the teacher invited the students to tape the appropriate pictures under the labels. Shown here are the four category titles, but each answer listed actually represents a picture the children classified. You may want to include a picture of some TV person that does not fit anywhere. You may also want to include a picture of someone such as a "Chan Clan" boy who might be placed appropriately in two categories, sons and detectives.

PICTURE TELL   Primary

Experience: Interpretation of pictures   Adapts to all ages

PICTURE TELL may be played in various ways related to TV. In almost every Sunday paper television section, in every **TV Guide,** on every newsstand, and on most coloring-book counters, there are pictures drawn from commercial television. Both TV photographs and illustrations are inexpensively handy. The following ideas are drawn from many versions of PICTURE TELL:

Place a picture of a television character on a colorful backing. Try to select a picture that shows this character and perhaps one other character doing something together. Their activity need not be one which they would do on the program. Ask the children to tell everything they can about the picture. List their observations on the board or a chart. Challenge them frequently by making statements yourself about the picture. Ask them to tell you if the statements you make really tell about the picture. Be sure that some of your statements **do not** describe the picture.

* * * * * * *

One teacher I know plays PICTURE TELL BECAUSE, another way to provide an experience in picture interpretation. She asks one child to supply the first part of a statement about a TV picture, for example, "Tarzan is swinging on that vine because _____ ." Other children are then invited to supply a logical ending based on information they derive from the picture. In this case, the ending chosen was "Boy and Cheetah are on the other side of the river calling for help." With older children you might wish to design your own set of statements about a TV picture you project using acetate transparencies, slides, or an opaque projector. One teacher makes up picture statements to go along with popular picture slide wheels about movies and television. In each case the student is asked to derive sensible answers based on his examination and interpretation of the picture.

* * * * * * *

PICTURE TELL WORDS may be played to provide experience in vocabulary building. One teacher placed the front cover of a Spiderman comic book on a large chart. "Spiderman" was at one time an extremely popular afternoon TV show. When this teacher worked with small groups, she asked the children to help her make lists of words that the picture suggested. Below are some of the word lists that came from those small group experiences in picture interpretation.

nouns	adjectives	verbs
Spiderman	fast	spin
policeman	strong	rob
net	quick	throw
car	mean	catch
bank	strange	call
foot	tall	
suit	red	
web	blue	
boots	black	
mask	thin	
	scary	

The teacher then encouraged these children to write or dictate a brief story that would tell about the cover using the word bank that had been previously developed.

POEM PLAY   Intermediate

Experience: Experimentation with   Adapts to all ages
                poetry forms

Many language arts and English textbooks suggest that students experiment with poetic forms and conventions. TV POEM PLAY has intrigued students and increased their repertoire of expressive forms. Here are some examples of TV-motivated POEM PLAY similar to those created by fourth graders:

couplet: If there is trouble the police chief sends
                  A message to the "Superfriends."

cinquain: John-Boy
                              Oldest son
                            Writes of family
                       Sensitive loving loyal smile
                                 Walton

limerick: There once was a stallion named Ed
                  Who talked as each day he was fed.
                      No one could believe it
                      That he could achieve it
                  "That's why it's a secret," Ed said.

triplet: We know about that horse.
                  It cannot talk of course.
                  We heard it from that source.

If you decide to POEM PLAY, do not forget to try other forms such as acrostics, sonnets, and haiku. Below is an example of TV haiku typical of those written by fifth graders. Notice that the notions of nature and contrasts expected in haiku are still present using TV subject matter.

                  Spring came early cool
                  To poor rural rough country,
                  Home sweet home Waltons.

My Own TV Notes:

We mostly ask and answer factual or literal questions. We know that in the classroom greater attention is generally paid to finding detail than to using more advanced mental processes. QUESTING provides a chance for us all to ask and answer higher order questions which, while more difficult, seem an intriguing challenge when posed in the setting of the well-known television data bank most children have acquired. I asked first-grade boys to answer questions such as these that follow (Potter, p. 171) and found that these young students could not only answer them but enjoyed doing this "thinking thing."

1. What would happen if one day some characters (people) from a television show you watch were on another show? What if Prince Planet were on the Flipper show?
Cognitive process: **extrapolation:** Bloom (pp. 90-96)

2. When Gomer Pyle says "Ga-ah-ah-ah-ah-lee," he means

_____ .

Cognitive process: **translation:** Bloom et al. (pp. 91-93)

3. If Flipper saw a boy get hurt in a swimming pool, she would

_____ .

Cognitive process: **extrapolation:** Bloom (pp. 95-96)

4. Who are the tallest (explain height with motion of hand) people on these six shows?
Cognitive process: **interpretation:** Bloom et al. (pp. 93-94)

*   *   *   *   *   *   *

I have found that most children love an appropriate level of THINKING GAME as described on pages 6 and 77. THINKING GAME entails many questions which tap advanced comprehension skills.

My Own TV Notes:

If youngsters are going to watch television, it is important that we prepare them to make better program selections by providing them experience with television previews and guides. In addition to the well-known **TV Guide**, there are many shopping center newspapers, daily newspapers, and Sunday sections which are resources for studying television programs. Most of these sources include times, dates, channels, and summaries. I find that many students need help in determining just how such a guide could be used. In addition the students need to be helped to read preview articles about special programs and the small summaries that usually accompany prime time show listings.

Using a daily newspaper I believe you will find time well spent helping the children figure out how to use the television section. Some help in vocabulary will be necessary such as "special," "rerun," "CBS," "NBC," "ABC," "repeat," "moves to," "interviews," "format," "narrates," and "1st of a 2-parter," to mention a very few TV terms.

One teacher I know asked the local newspaper to deliver enough papers for her whole sixth grade class one day. The first thing she asked her students to do was to use the front page index to locate the TV section. After all the students had found and turned to that page, the teacher encouraged a discussion which included:

1. What is the purpose of this guide or preview section?
2. What kinds of information can you locate here?
3. What parts of this section seem difficult to understand?
4. Where can we find evening programs?
5. On what channel would you expect to see _____ ?
6. If you watched _____ , what program would you miss?
7. Give the name of a program you have already seen. How can you explain this? (term: rerun/repeat, etc.)
8. What does "90 min." mean? Why would the guide include this information?
9. Find some information about a program you have seen. See whether you agree with what you read in this section about the program.

10. Find a time when there are two programs or more that you would like to see. Tell which one you are likely to select and why.
11. Think about your family's interest in television. Point out the programs that your folks watch together or individually. See if there is any time in which there might be a conflict of television interest.
12. Suggest some other kinds of information that you think might be included in this preview or guide.
13. Tell which things, if any, could be removed from the TV section you are studying without making the preview useless.

The ways that teachers can help children to interpret and better use the TV references are innumerable. One teacher told me that as a special treat in an older learning disability class, she invited her students to watch one-half hour of commercial television while they waited for their bus after school. The only condition the teacher placed on the students was that they had to plan among themselves which program to watch, using a TV preview and time schedule. They were expected to justify to the teacher why the group selected the program. They were also required to check the time of the program and to turn the set to the proper channel at that time. The teacher was astounded at the amount of logical discussion this TV reference generated among her students.

*　*　*　*　*　*　*

Still another way to use TV REFERENCE experience is to take a **TV Guide** apart and give each student a schedule page. I suggest that you also provide the student with a set of search questions and invite each youngster to use his **TV Guide** page to answer the questions. I have found that an individual ditto, an acetate on the overhead projector, and oral questioning all work well as ways to present the search questions. However, having considered the fact that most people use **TV Guide** rapidly and not in writing, I believe that oral questioning, sometimes with an informal time limit, may better simulate actual use and in that way help transfer of learning.

Here are some questions that I suggest for TV REFERENCE search questions, in **TV Guide:**

1. For what time period are the programs listed on your page?
2. What terms indicating time of day can you list that you find on either side of the page? _____ .

3. Name three programs that
   a. give you the same information _____ .
   b. could provide you with similar entertainment _____ .
   c. are animated _____ .
   d. you believe are not appropriate for young children _____ .
   e. might be described as adventure stories _____ .
   f. you would like a younger brother or sister to see _____ .
   g. would be of special interest to you _____ .
   h. you think will continue next season _____ .
4. Name two programs that you would want to see, which conflict as to time _____ . Describe the time conflict _____ (simultaneous/ overlap/ two-parter, etc.).
5. Which of the two conflicting programs will you probably choose to see? (A one-time special chosen over a very popular program which will be repeated in the spring, for example).
6. Tell us the meaning of the following terms or symbols:

(60 min.) _____ (Time approximate) _____
(Special) _____ (Smith/Reasoner) _____
(43) _____ (-Children) _____
(2 hrs.) _____ (6:45) _____
(-Variety) _____ (BW) _____

RIDDLING   Primary

Experience: Comprehension and   Adapts to all ages
           composition of riddles

Most students like guessing games. RIDDLING, using TV data, is a fascinating comprehension game. It is a learning experience in simple to complex clue synthesis. I played RIDDLING aloud with everyone in the class participating in listening. I did this before expecting any child to read or create riddles. The younger children were found to be quite factual and older children more inclined to subtlety and double meaning when concocting or considering clues.

Below are two riddles typical of those composed respectively by a second- and sixth-grade student:

I can live underwater.
I can swim fast.
I can call fish to help me.

I fight crime and pollution.
My name begins with A.
Who am I? I am _____ . (Aquaman from
"The Superfriends")

HANDSOME AND PRETTY
BAGPIPES AND GOLDEN GATE
SASSY HOMEMAKER
CRIME FIGHTERS
FAMILY LOVE
What show is this? _____ . ("MacMillan
and Wife")

* * * * * * *

Older students who enjoy RIDDLING might also like to try television crossword puzzles. I found that the one that appears weekly in **TV Guide** is reasonably easy and fun to do orally in class using an opaque projector. Another way to use this puzzle is to laminate it so that many students can try it. Students were eager to examine the answers which appeared in the **TV Guide** the next week.

SCIENCE SURVEY	Intermediate
Experience: Survey of TV science data	Adapts to all ages

Students can help themselves and teachers to learn the ways in which commercial television can be used to enhance science studies. A business and science librarian told me that the morning after a TV program based on scientific data has been shown, he receives numerous requests for material on the subject telecast. A teacher told me that she was amazed when her supposedly slow-learning class discussed pollution and antigravity with her, having heard those terms on Saturday's "Superfriends." Older students talk about moon walks, Sea- and Skylabs, brain waves, terminal disease, and transplants. When Jane Goodall's programs about primates were telecast, libraries were deluged with requests for books about all kinds of monkeys.

I invited children to participate in SCIENCE SURVEY. They were encouraged to notice and list everything they observed about commercial TV that might help them learn about science. Among the many items listed frequently were:

1. vocabulary: scientific terms in context

2. specials: documentaries, reports
3. concepts: pictorial and verbal meaning clues
4. news: announcements of concerns and breakthroughs
5. first-hand viewing: on the scene "moonwalking"
6. procedures: technical accounts; familiar treatments; symptoms; first aid
7. motivation: reading of additional material after telecast
8. topics: weather; ecology; animals; medicine; astronomy; health; mental health, social-medical problems; futurism; international work; models; communication; outer space; inner space; electronics; archaeology; zoology; geology; anthropology; manufacturing; refining; etc.

SCRIPTING   Older Primary

Experiences: Comprehension and   Adapts to older
            composition of
            script format

I can suggest two great ways to use TV scripts to help children read, interpret, and understand play format. I described the first reading of TV scripts in detail earlier on page 18. Teachers have used variations of it this year with nearly miraculous results in both reading interest and quantity of material read.

                    *   *   *   *   *   *   *

Writing scripts has also been successful as a motivator and skill builder. This version of SCRIPTING is described in detail as a variation of I AM AUTHOR, an experience found on pages 43-46 of this book.

SHOW SORT   Intermediate

Experiences: Identification and   Adapts to all ages
            classification of show types

With this TV experience, teachers can help children to understand the special relationships involved in classification. Children can also experience the added dimension of determining categories. You may already have used PICTURE SORT described on page 57 as a kind of readiness for this thinking activity. You may also want to use THINKING GAME, page 77, as the lead-in for this experience.

In SHOW SORT children are invited to dictate a list of at least 25 TV programs. Everyone will probably want to contribute, which is great! The name of the programs are listed on the board in the order they are suggested. The students are then encouraged to examine the list and suggest the various types of programs they think are represented on the list. These suggested types of programs become the labels for the classification chart experience.

I observed that the children discussed each program type and came to an agreement as to what a show must be like to be placed in a particular category. The children then told the teacher in which category each show listed belonged. Below is one partially completed class list typical of those I have seen. There was much worthwhile discussion about placement.

comedy	animal story	cartoon
"Rhoda"	"Lassie's Rescue Rangers"	"Pink Panther"
"Three Stooges"		"Scooby-Doo"
"Flintstones"	"Run, Joe, Run"	"Yogi's Gang"

family	real life	make-believe
"Good Times"	"Adam-12"	"Star Trek"
"Sunshine"	"Emergency"	"Shazam"

SPIN-OFFS   Primary

Experience: Character/setting/time   Adapts to all ages
                    inference

From the time Grannie Clampett on "Beverly Hillbillies" began to doctor country folks on other programs such as "Green Acres" and "Petticoat Junction," children have been noting with pleasure the "mixing" of program details which I shall call "spin-offs" in TV writing. Such writing required the script people to use some advanced levels of inference, an important comprehension skill. They not only had to know the details about the characters on one show, but also had to know well the personalities on the other shows. Then, using what details they knew, they had to infer what would happen if a character from one show appeared as that same character in a different TV story. [In the new story Grannie would have to behave as naturally on the "Green Acres" farm with Miss Gabor as on the "Beverly Hillbillies" set with her "real" TV family.]

Some visiting of characters has often led to spin-off programs.

For example, Gomer left Mayberry for his own highly successful program as a Marine. Maude's maid went home to her own program. Mary Tyler Moore's friend, Rhoda, went back to New York and was married into her own TV show format.

I asked the children to play SPIN-OFFS in the form of a lively discussion requiring inference. I began with some of the sample questions listed below:

1. What is TV visiting? (I helped them define this.)
2. What is a TV spin-off? (I helped this definition too.)
3. Why would a TV scriptwriter make up a spin-off? (prior success; audience response, etc.)
4. Who visited on Scooby-Doo's program? (Phyllis Diller, Don Knotts, Sonny and Cher, among others, and all in cartoon form!) Why do you think that the writers picked these stars as visitors? (character personality; setting of "Scooby-Doo;" creation of interest; fun; humor, etc.) "The Partridge Family" appeared live for a while. Why do you imagine that the writers then made it into a cartoon? (Stars were no longer available; cartoons can do more flexible things, etc.)
5. Why does the new "Partridge Family" cartoon program take place in the future?
6. What other programs do you remember that were once seen with live actors and are now seen in cartoon form? ("I Dream of Jeannie," "My Favorite Martian," and "Gilligan's Island.")
7. Why were "Devlin" and "Superfriends" in cartoon form from the beginning? (Both shows required stunts too difficult to stage with live actors, including, for example, motorcycle tricks and humans flying.)

I found that, with a little oral experience, second-grade children were able to discuss the notions of visiting and spin-offs with little difficulty.

* * * * * * *

Older children might of course be asked more complex questions. I have encouraged earnest conversations with all of the sample questions listed below:

1. Why do you imagine that Rhoda was chosen as the character for a spin-off TV program by that same name? (Possibilities of character; well-liked by public; independent nature or humor, etc.)

2. Why did the writers for "The Mary Tyler Moore Show" **not** do a program called "Ted?" (The inept anchorman Ted Baxter may be so real to audience that he could not be a star type; Ted is more like a supporting character, etc.)
3. Could there be other spin-offs from this program? If so, name the spin-off.
4. From what program do you imagine "Superfriends" was a spin-off? ("Batman," "Superman," etc.)

* * * * * * *

You may enjoy the application of inferential thinking to the following version of SPIN-OFFS.

I invited students of many ages to suggest logical spin-off programs derived from the following TV shows:

"Tarzan" (They suggested ape and wild boy stories.)
"The Waltons" (I was told that we could spin-off stories about each child's growing up; one child suggested a flashback on the grandparents' early years!)
"Land of the Lost"
"Chico and the Man"
"The Carol Burnett Show"
"That's My Mama"

As students explained their reasons for each suggested spin-off, others listened appreciatively and with surprising interest in agreeing or disagreeing. It was a very pleasant teaching moment for me when the students "held" the continuing discussion themselves, often with such seriousness that it was hard to believe that they were not the scriptwriters of the newly suggested programs. What good thinking the students were enjoying!

SPORTING	Intermediate
Experience: Comprehension of TV sports coverage	Adapts to all ages

So much commercial TV time is devoted to sports information that SPORTING became a fine vehicle for many exciting comprehension experiences. I found that students enjoyed following sports on television, writing to sports figures, reporting on a variety of sports programs, discussing the Olympics, predicting contest outcomes, studying game fundamentals, and developing skill at recording and reading sports data, among many other language activities. The sports figures are of particular interest as a language stimulus.

Made so popular by television, sports stars have become the subject for study in several classrooms. Some students have enjoyed preparing and updating collections of clippings about particular sports personalities. Other students enjoy reading these scrapbooks or pressbooks. Some students, having read many articles and supplementary books about contemporary sports figures, decided to create biographies drawn from their studies. One student intends to submit her finished work to the tennis star about whom she wrote. She is hoping that her TV tennis heroine will read the biography and then tell the young author how accurately she has written.

* * * * * * *

Students I know are also learning to write and deliver sports news and commentary. Some classes are learning to make oral play-by-play reports. One boy is even trying to develop speaking ability as a "color man," the person whose style and humor adds a knowledgeable insight to the report of the contest as we hear it described and watch it. Just telling these sports deliveries apart proved interesting to some students. I have heard some fascinating discussions among students about the styles of TV sportscasters and editorialists. You may imagine that Howard Cosell and Heywood Hale Broun pose quite different sports personalities to examine. Finally, I also know of two classes where students watched the TV coverage of a game and compared notes in detail with those students who had only read a newspaper account of the game. They also compared descriptions with those students who had been in the stadium.

Although I do admit that boys seemed to enjoy SPORTING more than did girls in general, girls' interest in TV sports and sports in general is growing more evident daily, thanks to TV sports personalities such as Billie Jean King, Chris Evert, and the Olympian gymnasts. I find that many girls really enjoy watching professional football both in person and at home on TV.

STORY PARTS   Intermediate

Experience: Identification of   Adapts to all ages
             story parts

Children need experience with recognizing and identifying the plot line of stories. This skill enables youngsters to better understand what they read and better plan the stories they write. I asked students to classify mixed-up TV story parts within the following categories: What is the problem? How is the problem solved? How does the story end?

The teacher invited oral student responses at first. First he read the three story fragments. After providing this listening experience, he invited the students to locate the story parts. The students enjoyed this. Then the teacher took dictation on the board from class members who thought of other programs and who, with the help of friends, again classified the parts.

Below are two samples of TV stories in which students have successfully identified the story parts. One fragment is drawn from an actual television drama, "Apple's Way." The other is from "Mod Squad," created using known story details. Students can write about TV stories they have seen. These student-created materials can be used for further STORY PARTS.

When he heard that the developers were going to cut down the tree, Mr. Apple tried to get the mayor and others to stop the construction men. When he could not get any help, Mr. Apple climbed into the tree. Do you recall the show? He refused to get down. The police came. The mayor came. A hundred interested townspeople came. Some people climbed up into the tree with Mr. Apple. At last the protests brought results. The property owners decided to build somewhere else. Mr. Apple came down from the tree. This is the very tree here. Isn't it pretty? We like to think we have a beautiful park.

Link had been gone for several hours when we suddenly realized how late it was. He was never so late before. Pete and I finally decided to go looking for Link. I am sure glad we did. Someone had tied him up in the car. Just as we found Link, Pete heard a noise. I saw someone slip around the corner of the building. Could we catch him? Pete went one way. I went the other. We managed to surprise the man. Pete and I tied him up. Later we found out that the man was wanted for questioning in a bank robbery. The funny thing was the man thought Link was someone else. We caught him by mistake!

The students had no difficulty identifying the problem Mr. Apple had. They easily pointed out how the problem was solved. They were less certain on how the stories really ended. One student was certain that all stories have a completely happy ending. As the STORY PART experience continued, he was able to see that the story is usually ended with a neat solution, but not always a happy one.

Students had more difficulty identifying the problem in the "Mod Squad" story fragment. There was a dispute about the problem. Some students believed that Link's absence was the problem. Others contended that the robbery suspect was the problem. They did agree, though, on the solution and the ending.

*   *   *   *   *   *   *

Another version of STORY PARTS is STORY PARTS REWRITE. Students are invited to use their imaginations in creating alternative story parts to replace those parts already examined. STORY PARTS REWRITE is effectual because it is fun and demands good thinking. I found that students thought this experience challenging and often hilarious! Each newly created story fragment must be justified by the writers in relationship to the two original story parts.

My Own TV Notes:

SUPERNATURAL/SCI-FI	Intermediate
Experience: An analysis of supernatural and science-fiction story elements	Adapts older

---

Many people are fascinated by the macabre or futuristic story. The popularity of both supernatural and science-fiction tales has been recognized for centuries. We well recall Poe, Verne, and Wells. We will not soon forget Stoker's **Dracula** and Shelley's **Frankenstein.** Many of us also remember the radio programs called "Lights Out";

"Inner Sanctum Mysteries," with its creaking door; and "Hermit's Cave," all "tales well-calculated to keep you in suspense," as was the slogan of "Suspense." I could name numerous movies which captivated us all in shivering interest. From this it is obvious that TV is certainly not the only medium with supernatural or science fiction stories. However, since TV is so popular, it seems a natural source of data which might help students better understand our interest in the strange and fantastic. Some TV programs which represent this fascination are "Captain Video" (a very early sci-fi); "Star Trek"; "Voyage to the Bottom of the Sea"; "Bewitched"; "Lost in Space"; and "Twilight Zone."

I encouraged students to examine the elements of the unusual found on TV to explore the way that the imaginative creations of men seem to stir our own imaginations. In SUPERNATURAL/SCI-FI we invited students to try:

1. Comparing the TV presentation with the original book; for example, **Dracula** and **Frankenstein**.
2. Classifying programs as to type, such as science-fiction: future; machines; invasion; creatures; supernatural: ghosts; superstitions; creatures;
3. Assessing why "Bewitched," "Sabrina," and "My Favorite Martian" are funny.
4. Deciding why "Dracula," "Creature Feature," or "Twilight Zone" are frightening.
5. Attempting to decide why "Star Trek" was a five-year voyage and why that program, now in reruns and animation, still has an enormous following.
6. Examining the appeal of "Jeannie," and "The Ghost and Mrs. Muir."
7. Identifying some of the strange creatures; for example, genies, witches, warlocks, demons, vampires, ghosts, werewolves, and misshapen dwarfs.
8. Comparing some of these creatures to those we have seen in literature, such as Caliban in Shakespeare's **Tempest** and his three witches in **Macbeth;** Polyphemus in the stories about Ulysses; Gollum in Tolkien's **The Fellowship of the Ring;** or Grendel in **Beowulf.**
9. Deciding what techniques writers use to create apprehension in us; for example, achieving and sustaining suspense through violin music or slowly-delivered dialogue, while we hear strange, fearful sounds or the threatened approach of some dreadful creature coming out of a stormy night.

I have found older students quite interested in analyzing the supernatural programs that they view to the point where some of them found great glee in predicting what would happen next in the shows. They had "discovered" stock elements such as lightning and old houses and the foreshadowing which lines like, "It is a good thing that IT cannot escape the metal cage it's in," have for the story's action.

As you use SUPERNATURAL/SCI-FI, remember that it is the same kind of study that famous and frightening authors underwent in their own times to create for us the stories we still read with fear. The late Rod Serling's imaginative career depended on his ability to stir us. With experience, encourage students to write paragraphs which set us tingling. My only reservation is that you play down the extremely grotesque and shocking such as the material they may suggest a la "The Night Stalker." There is so much to be learned about basic suspense, good story line, and irony, that there is little reason to include the quicker, less clever, less costly effects such as sudden bloody scenes and suggestions of mad sadism. You are advised to provide great and traditional ghost, suspense and science-fiction stories for analysis. This will also offset the cheaper works which often find their way into all media.

SURPRISE SPELL	Intermediate/Secondary
Experience: Use of spelling words in sentences	Adapts to older primary

I found that a waning interest in the accurate use of spelling words in sentences was turned into a zealous experience when I tried SURPRISE SPELL with sixth graders. First I invited the children to dictate a list of ten to fifteen television programs. I wrote the names of the programs on the board. Then the students were asked to volunteer sentences that would incorporate at least one spelling word AND some data from one of the TV programs. The results were delightful. One condition of acceptance for any sentence was that the spelling word be sensibly connected with the program data. After the class had caught the idea of SURPRISE SPELL, I invited them to try their own sentences. The room became silent as each student tried this writing experience, the quiet broken only by an occasional chuckle from someone enjoying his own cleverness. After the students had completed written sentences, many volunteered to share their sentences with their attentive peers. The teacher of this class used SPELLING SURPRISE weekly, continuing to note the remarkable interest in spelling and comprehension generated by this experience. Below are some sentences typical of those written by students. The spelling words were underlined.

Of <u>course</u> there is a program about Christy Love.
Chico had to wash his <u>friend's</u> shirt.
Krocker <u>said</u> that the house over <u>there</u> belonged to Kojak.
<u>That</u> is Scooby-Doo's footprint.
I <u>like</u> "Night Stalker." He saw a man walk <u>through</u> a wall.
Jethro <u>often</u> says funny things.
"<u>Stop</u> that, Dingbat."

More sentences may be seen in the work pictured on page 76.

More sentences may be seen in the work pictured on page 76.

*   *   *   *   *   *   *

Two versions of SPELLING SURPRISE involving more difficult skills are as follows:

1. Students are invited to write a summary of a TV program they have seen incorporating all of their spelling words.
2. Students are encouraged to use content area vocabulary which they are expected to know as in social studies or science and to incorporate it sensibly with television programs. Example: Yesterday Fred Flintstone traveled through a <u>historical</u> time tunnel. Along the way from <u>B.C.</u> to <u>A.D.</u> he met many of the <u>figures</u> known to be <u>pioneers</u> and <u>patriarchs</u> of our present republic.

This experience is known to motivate reluctant students. However, the eventual goal would still be to use these terms in the original contexts of their settings, such as a story about the way this country began.

THAT MADE THIS HAPPEN   Primary

Experience: Development awareness of   Adapts to older
              cause and effect relationship

Ask the children to tell you the most important thing that happened in each of ten different TV programs. List the ten happenings on the board under the heading **this.** Then ask the class to tell you why each important event happened. Ask, "What made this happen?" List a suggested cause for each event in a column to the left of the **this**

Clarence   March 6, 1975

1 Evel Knievel is eating his dinner.

2 Shazam is going to ride in a boat.

3 I will rain on Speed racer.

4 Costello put on his coat.

5 We read a Story about The Land

of the Lost.

6 The Three Stooges Caught a goat

7 Shazam is cooKing the meat.

8 Lucy picKed up the mail.

from the mail box,

9 Speed Buggy tooK the mail.

10 The Apes wait for the man.

column and next to the appropriate effect listed there. Label the cause column **That.** Next, reinforce the temporal-spatial notion indicated by reading from left to right (earlier to later) by saying with the children, "That made this happen." Say this while pointing first to the **That** column and next to the matching event in the **this** list. The following is an example of one second grade's rendition of THAT MADE THIS HAPPEN:

76   Many Other Channels

That (made)	**this** (happen.)
The spooky man jumped out.	Scooby-Doo was shaking.
Link was very late.	Pete and Julie were unhappy.
The apes got the man.	The astronaut was in a cage.
Billy said, "Shazam."	Captain Marvel came.
Aquaman cleaned up the red tide.	The water looked pretty again. The fish were all right.

* * * * * * *

For an oral matching activity, you could list the That column ideas out of order, asking students to select and justify the correct matching of causes and effects. Still another way to play this experience is to place the data suggested by the children on five-by-eight-inch cards, preferably typing the statements with a primary typewriter. This could become an independent matching activity for a learning center. However, an answer key should then be provided with the cards to make the game self-checking.

* * * * * * *

Another extension of this experience is the year-long accumulation of different and updated **That** and **this** matches. Some children might wish to illustrate their cause-effect match by adding a pictorial aid for less-able youngsters.

THINKING GAME   Intermediate

Experience: Introduction to varied   Adapts to all ages
            word and comprehension skills

This experience is an extension of THINKING GAME as first described on page 6. THINKING GAME is an exploratory experience for you and the students. I will not repeat the initial directions here, but instead list other ways we have played this experience to advantage. The children were delighted to extend the game. We could have gone on for hours, but the regular teacher came back from her meeting and we had to stop. Some of the experiences listed below were suggested by them as we gathered our things and left the room.

Looking toward the board I asked sixth-grade students:

1. Tell me all the shows that are about families.
2. Tell us which shows are about contemporary families. Which families apparently lived in an earlier day?
3. Which program is really the story of one of the children?
4. In which program is there usually a cause for which everyone fights?
5. Think of two programs which take place in inner space; Outer space.
6. Which programs are plausible? Which would be impossible?
7. Name a program which you believe to be technically clever. Why?
8. Which program gives girls a realistic modern role? Which ones don't?
9. On which of these programs do you find serious conflicts which might face the average person?
10. We notice that there are many detective programs listed. Why so?
11. Why do you think there are so many crime stories right now?
12. How do these shows differ? How are they the same?
13. How do these detectives differ? Contrast Kojak with Columbo.
14. If you were writing a television program, which type would interest you more—fantasy-animated or human-plausible?
15. If you were to place these programs in categories, what would the labels be?

*   *   *   *   *   *   *

A labeling version of the game was then used in which the teacher and the students were coequal to play. One person began by announcing a very brief and hopefully clever label, for example, Girl's Lib. A student suggested that "Get Christy Love" or "The Mary Tyler Moore Show" would bear that label. The next label was provided by that student with the logical answer. Here are some labels suggested by children and matched with possible answers:

Special Training	"The Rookies"
Older Detective	"Barnaby Jones"
Hero Hall	"Superfriends"

Atomic Power	"Prince Planet"
Glub!	"Voyage to the Bottom of the Sea"
Wiggle	"Bewitched"
Ears	"Star Trek"
Family Way Out	"Lost in Space"
Insect	"Spiderman"
Lollipop	"Kojak"
6 Kids	"Brady Bunch"
B.C.	"Flintstones"
Fat Friend	"Jeannie"
Second Chance	"Mod Squad"
Fast Transportation	"Chopper One"
Soapbox	"Apple's Way"

*   *   *   *   *   *   *

Another version of THINKING GAME may be inviting the students to write clues from simpler versions to complex without giving answers. Students hear clues aloud and try to guess.

*   *   *   *   *   *   *

Still another version is DO NOT LEAVE THE NAMES OF PRO-GRAMS ON BOARD THINKING GAME. As the students became more accustomed to this thought game, I found I could erase the list of programs from the board and add a memory bank aspect to the experience.

*   *   *   *   *   *   *

Organize teams who devise clever short clues for the class. Keep a year-long running team record on clues and stumping. I invited students to put clues up on the bulletin board, leaving a box for answers.

* * * * * * *

Use the whole notion as an attention-getting idea, while waiting in lines, as a filler, driving on field trips, etc. The students already have the guessing data with them. Use it effectively in THINKING GAME.

* * * * * * *

This primary version of THINKING GAME has been an unqualified success with very young children in first grade and with slow learners. Instead of listing programs, the teacher invited each child to draw a large picture of one of his favorite TV programs. She then took the pictures and cut them out, placing these pictorial "clouds" on a large bulletin board. Under each picture the teacher placed the name of the program in manuscript print large enough to read from seats or standing near board. As you can see in the photograph on page 79, a child went to the TV bulletin board and located data to answer questions such as:

1. Show "Planet of the Apes." (Use of picture clues)
2. Name the programs where an animal is the star. (analysis, classification)
3. Which programs could be a true story? Which are make-believe?
4. Which programs are about problems? (analysis; interpretation)
5. Show three programs that begin with the same sound as (summer?) (comparison)
6. Give the name of a program that is **not** on the bulletin board that begins like Superman. (missing details)
7. Show a program that has two words in its title and also the little word (and) in a bigger title word. ("Gilligan's Island")

THIS IS TO THAT   Primary

Experience: Recognition of analogy   Adapts to all ages
                relationship

I have found that children have little school experience with analogies. THIS IS TO THAT provided students with some entertaining oral experience by using analogies drawn from television data. I placed the sample analogies on charts and invited both small and large groups of children to examine them and to determine answers. Of course, the children were asked to explain their decisions. The relationships they explained were not always those I chose, but their judgment was surprisingly sound once they became aware of the way analogies generally "work." The children will need help in figuring out the first line relationship, to name that relationship, and then to decide the logical answer. You will need to establish also the spoken pattern THIS IS TO THAT. You might place the analogies on charts in the following manner:

THIS	(IS TO)	THAT
Shazam		Billy
	(AS)	
spinach	(IS TO)	(Popeye)

The cause and effect relationship of note here is that the word "Shazam" turns Billy into powerful Captain Marvel, analogous to spinach, which when eaten by Popeye, makes him powerful.

Other analogies I have used include the following data and relationships:

Captain Marvel: Billy/ Superman: Clark Kent (after-before link)

cave: "Land of the Lost"/ bottle: "I Dream of Jeannie" (home-title link)

sky: Superman/ ocean: Aquaman (habitat-dweller link)

Elmer Fudd: Bugs Bunny/ Wiley Coyote: Roadrunner (pursuer to sly pursued)

* * * * * * *

And with older students I have tried analogies similar to the following samples:

Skipper: Gilligan/ The Man: Chico   (friendly boss-employee link)

Columbo: meticulous/ Kojak: disheveled (opposite state of grooming)

raincoat: Columbo/ lollipop: Kojak (eccentricity match)

Theresa Merritt is to Clifton Davis as
Esther Rolle is to Jimmie Walker. (names of real actresses and actors who play mother-son roles in "That's My Mama," and "Good Times" as Mama, Clifton, Florida, and J.J., in that order)

My Own TV Notes:

TIE-INS

Experience: Application of reading
skills, self-chosen high
interest TV related material

Many teachers have told me that students are now reading TV-related books and magazines with zeal. On a recent trip to an airport newsstand, I was able to count forty different magazines in some way related to TV. I found many paperback books entirely devoted to TV data such as soap operas, commercials, doctors, stars, and program content. At one store I examined book racks and quickly located fifteen different titles related to TV programs. For example, school librarians are telling me that they cannot keep enough of the very popular Laura Ingalls Wilder books available on the shelf. At the bookstore I heard the same thing about the Wilder paperbacks. It seems that since the TV adaptation of the Wilder book **The Little House on the Prairie** became popular, so have the original books in the series that the author wrote about her life. As always, people read what they want to read.

You may be interested in the following list of TV-related paperback books that I found readily available at newsstands:

THE LITTLE HOUSE
  ON THE PRAIRIE
Wilder Harper
(other series titles available)

PLANET OF THE APES
Effinger Award Books

TV MOVIES
Maltin Signet

THE WORLD OF STAR TREK
Gerrold Ballantine

A GIRL NAMED SOONER
Clauser Avon Books

THE AUTOBIOGRAPHY OF
  MISS JANE PITTMAN
Gaines Dial Press

THE BOOK ON HOW TO
  WRITE FOR TV
Whitfield/Roddenberry Ballantine

STAR TREK: LOG ONE
Foster Bantam

There were twenty-four titles available in this series of which I list one:

TARZAN OF THE APES
Burroughs   Ballantine

For those of you that are concerned with the reading level of the books listed, the next paperbacks listed were written for about fourth-grade readers. When these titles were presented to intermediate and older, more reluctant readers, students eagerly read them.

TV TIME '74
Herz   Scholastic Book Services
FLIP WILSON CLOSE UP
Hudson   Scholastic Book Services
TV STARS of '73
Hudson   Scholastic Book Services

Also available from this publisher are books about Bill Cosby, the Osmond Brothers, the Jackson Five, and TV comedians. All of these books have photographs of the stars at work and play and are written in an informal manner and from the point of view of an interviewer.

There are many TV-related books available. These tie-ins prove an exciting, alternative motivation for reading, one which the reluctant reader cannot resist.

TIME-LINE	Intermediate
Experience: Analysis of time sequence	Adapts to all ages

Several teachers tell me that they used TV to help children understand time sequence. A time line was drawn the full length of the chalkboard. The teachers then asked their classes to name TV programs and justify placement of each program on the time line. The reasons given for locating a program at first related to the present time. After a while, the teachers said there was productive controversy over placement of a show with regard to other programs' placement. One teacher remarked that after she tried this TV experience with her students, the students had less difficulty creating time lines for social studies projects.

Here is an example of one TV TIME-LINE:

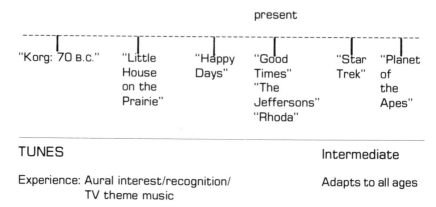

present

| "Korg: 70 B.C." | "Little House on the Prairie" | "Happy Days" | "Good Times" "The Jeffersons" "Rhoda" | "Star Trek" | "Planet of the Apes" |

TUNES   Intermediate

Experience: Aural interest/recognition/   Adapts to all ages
            TV theme music

One music teacher used TV successfully to foster children's attention to musical memory. She taped the theme music from the programs "Gilligan's Island," "The Little House on the Prairie," "Can-
non," and "Flintstones," then learned to play the melodies on the
piano for her own children. Next she presented the theme music
excerpts to a fourth-grade class by playing each tune on the bells,
and asked the students to identify the tunes. Not only did they do so
quickly, but with great gusto, begging for more TUNES. She
teacher was also pleased when the children literally insisted on
singing the songs they had identified such as the song from "Speed
Racer." Where attention had once lagged, this enterprising music
teacher had rejuvenated a musical memory lesson in a refreshing
manner. The children then enjoyed identifying songs they had already learned in school.

*   *   *   *   *   *   *

You might wish to use this same listening experience with younger
children. Select only those theme songs that are drawn from programs which you think young children watch and from those which
are viewed at hours appropriate to small youngsters. The following
programs have catchy tunes as theme music and exemplify the
suggestions made above: "Scooby-Doo," "The Waltons," "I Dream
of Jeannie," "Speed Racer," and "Popeye Show." You may want to
choose from many more programs viewed in your own area.

*   *   *   *   *   *   *

Another way to use TV theme music is to consider the lyrics. Ask the students to dictate, tape, or write the lyrics for TV theme music they know. Younger and less able children will feel more comfortable dictating the words to you or singing the songs on tape. You may find that they have never paid much attention to the lyrics and must re-sing the complete song each time until they have all the lines dictated. The same may be true for older or more able youngsters, even though they may be writing the lyrics by themselves. You may wish to tape the TV songs they sing and later transcribe the words. In any case, I suggest that you make dittos of these words or at least enough pages (to save paper) for one TV THEME SONG BOOK. This student-created book based on children's command of TV material may become very special reading material. And it would be one book to which students might add as programs appear and disappear. (This book might be to some students what a weekly rock tune sheet is to them.)

*　*　*　*　*　*　*

A spin-off idea from the use of TV theme lyrics might be a discussion about the purpose these themes or their lyrics serve as part of the program on which they are heard. For example, in the opening theme music of both "The Beverly Hillbillies" and "Gilligan's Island," the theme music lyrics told us the entire idea of series, the locales, and the characters we would grow to know in these ever-popular programs. A similar statement may be made about "All in the Family," except that in that case, the lyricist was relating the attitude and humor that would lend that program its famous flavor.

*　*　*　*　*　*　*

TV-TUNES may also be used in conjunction with studying commercials. Some of the commercial melodies have become well-known and, replaced with non-commercial lyrics, widely enjoyed. However, you might ask children to consider the reasons why such short commercial messages often include music and lyrics. In preparation for this activity, ask yourself this question: what was the commercial tune you once heard on each of the long-gone **radio** programs, "Let's Pretend" and "The FBI in Peace and War?" If you haven't the slightest idea, then you are younger than I. But if you are immediately able to sing a strand or two of a hot cereal or hand soap commercial, you may begin to understand how TV commercial melodies make a lasting impression on one's memory. You younger readers may recall the same impact when two huge soft drink companies each produced TV commercial tunes that rapidly became famous songs about peace.

We cannot assume that children know how to use TV. It has taken me a long time to figure out positive TV use for myself. When I asked second-grade children how they used TV, they first answered in terms of educational television, which is fine. I am glad that youngsters recognize what they can learn from programming designed for that purpose. However, when I inquired what use they made of programs they watched at home, they found it very difficult to answer. Some children mentioned counting and letters, again re-

Josefina March 7, 1975

I Do not want to see spooky things.
I Do not like to see somebody shoot a gun.
I like to see the Flintstones.
and I like to see lucy. I like to
see pritt be witch. and I like to
see jeanie.
* from t.v. I learned to do funny
things from the three stooges

Josefina March 13, 1975
These are the ways I use TV:
I learned about Sports and funny things. and about
the three Stooges. and the Flintones when he does
something wrong he tell the truth.

lated to public broadcasting programs. But some youngsters, as evidenced from the unedited writing (in the top portion of photographs) on pages 86 and 87, were not able to tell much about TV use. Note that children recalled learning about animals and funny things to do. But one child expressed the more typical response, "I don't know about (how) TV can help me at school." Yet within a week, this child was able to write a far more discerning comment on TV use, asked to consider her handwriting, but still writing on her own and obviously unedited.

Henry

How can TV help you at school. I learned about snakes.

Henry   March 13, 1975
These are the ways I use TV:
I learned about sports. I learn about basketball. I saw the Milwaukee bucks. I learned about words like zoom bionic incomplete like in football. People teaching people things I see on TV. Little house on the prairie Tells me about things in the old days.

I included the before and after pictures of the children's remarks because I wanted you to see how an awareness of TV use can be fostered. This was accomplished by means of an experience provided them called USE TRANSFER. Children were shown twenty-one mounted pictures clipped from magazines. Each picture, they were told, represented one way that some people use television. As each picture was presented, the children decided the TV use they thought was being depicted. They were enthusiastic once they realized that the pictures represented general uses, rather than only objects shown in them. For example, rain clouds did not mean to use TV for rain clouds, but for weather information. The children finally listed twenty-one major uses for television as shown below.

1. news
2. weather
3. sports
4. science
5. ecology
6. animals
7. other children
8. other places
9. words
10. things to do
11. places to go
12. machines (use; operation)
13. shopping (prices, products)
14. consumerism (propaganda)
15. how things work
16. music
17. fun
18. old days
19. current events
20. people relations
21. ideas

Not only could the children identify uses, but they also began to give examples of programs which they could use in these ways. I wonder if the creators of "The Six Million Dollar Man" realize that children said their show could be used to learn vocabulary! After this USE TRANSFER experience, I asked the children to write about ways that they actually use television. The results, as you see in the bottom part of each picture (pages 89 and 90), speak for themselves. On page 91 third graders told me about USE TRANSFER with pictures.

Of course, I cannot guarantee that USE TRANSFER in the classroom will make the child use TV well. I do believe that for the children who try USE TRANSFER the experience may pose a beginning lesson in TV criticism. One child who participated in USE TRANSFER told me that she talked about this experience with her parents. This is the same child who informed me that she is making a list of all the animals that she views on television. She plans to bring the list to school then and share with us what she has learned about each animal.

Many Other Channels

Dolores

T.V. can help me at school

My techer and mother and Farher

**
I don't now about T.V. can help me at school.

Dolores   March 13, 1975
These are the ways I use T.V.
I use T.V. to learn about sports
about baseball like baseball
players play basball and I
Learned aboat word like Systems.
And I learn about news like a
police he got shoot by a crook.
They got the crook

VAL-YOU

Experience: Recognition of values   Adapts to all ages

Every time children watch television they see values represented in action, plots, and characterization. While we are still not certain exactly what values, if any, we acquire from television, we can be sure that this medium is loaded with value data which we can study. As teachers, we are expected to help children clarify and examine the values that motivate human beings. We want to help students recognize values, to determine how values are acquired, and to

> Eric   March 7, 1975
> IN a good move at the
> good part of a move it trun
> black.
> on a move they realy have
> move stars an I like to meet
> a move star I want to be a
> move star.
> ★ from tv I have learned to learned about animals
>
> Eric   March 13, 1975
> These are the ways I use TV:
> I learn about a way to use tv.
> I learn about old days like
> Mickey Mouse westerndays and
> like the Waltons and Lucy and
> Snow White and like President Kenne-
> dy.

realize how decisions are made based on what people believe to be important. We hope that students will begin to examine their own values.

Discussions about values stemming from TV examples and children's experiences have proved a successful way to recognize and note the power of values. I call this experience VAL-YOU. When I used it, I invited the students to consider the following two questions:

1. What five reasons can you list that John-Boy Walton might walk to a town ten miles away? (Parents ill; save gasoline; keep a promise)
2. What kind of future is Sam on "Sunshine" planning for his child Jill? (happy experiences; always home; loving home)

I asked students to label the values their answers in parentheses suggest. For question one they named family love, thrift, and dependability. For question two they provided happiness, responsibility, and love. They then discussed how Sam and John-Boy had acquired their respective values, trying to determine when each character might have decided these values were important. Were these values learned from parents, friends, happy or sad experiences? Students easily identified some value-learning with their own learning experiences.

Students were also encouraged to note how values motivate

behavior. Discussion included examples ranging from why people really stop at red traffic lights to why television commercials are as they are. One small group of students decided that John-Boy learned to value loyalty because he valued history books and had read about Abraham Lincoln. They suggested that John-Boy Walton valued loyalty. That is why he walked ten miles to keep a promise. They also noted that John-Boy probably did not value foot rest as much as loyalty.

* * * * * * *

In another version of VAL-YOU, I asked students to keep track of events or behavior on TV programs which bother them. They analyzed some of these events to determine the value conflict causing their annoyance. Sometimes students told me that a character they liked just "would not act that way." When I examined the way the character had behaved I usually found, as did the children, that the character held different values than I had first thought. One student remarked that she had sympathized with a robber when she at first heard his tale of woe. However, later news showed her that the man held no regard for human life. He did not value people.

Similarly, I found that children connected their own values with characters and behavior they approved. It was not long before the TV values discussion branched off into values of country and community, more specifically to the relationship between littering and community values. The values discussed included beauty, responsibility, and hope. The students decided that litterbugs do not value health and pretty surroundings. Polluters, they conjectured, must not value themselves!

Try VAL-YOU as an alternative way to examine values in common settings.

My Own TV Notes:

VOWEL WOW	Primary
Experience: Auditory recognition/ classification of vowel sounds in words	Adapts older

---

Many Other Channels

Children and teachers may be refreshed by this alternative way to review vowel sounds. VOWEL WOW proved that children were eager to redirect their attention to this very precise vowel skill.

One day VOWEL WOW was used in this manner: I asked the children to name as many TV programs as they could within five minutes, then listed the names on the board. Next I placed five vowels on the board with a key word for sound next to the vowel that indicated whether the vowel was long or short. The key words I used were TV words, all indicating short vowels—short **a,** B**a**tman; short **e,** "G**e**t Smart"; short **i,** **I**nch-High; short **o,** "M**o**d Squad"; and short **u,** H**u**ckleberry Hound. I then invited the students to classify the listed TV items by vowel sounds. They did well and listened very closely to the vowel sounds in the names of their favorite TV characters and shows as I printed their suggestions below each sample vowel.

*   *   *   *   *   *   *

I have had VOWEL WOW success with older students when I invited them to classify TV vowel words on a ditto. I asked for very particular sorting, such as variant forms of **a,** as in "**A**stroboy," "Speed R**a**cer," "G**e**t Smart." Imagine the possibilities for variant vowel **o** in the one title, "V**o**yage t**o** the B**o**ttom **o**f the Sea." I have never found another vowel experience that motivated children to ask to continue as in the case of VOWEL WOW. For this reason, you may want to try VOWEL WOW for its extensive aid in learning precise sound skills.

WHAT'S NEXT?	Primary
Experience: Placement of events in sequence	Adapts to all ages

Invite the children to name four programs which most of them have seen recently. With each of four smaller groups of children, determine the actual sequence of major events in each program. Prepare a ditto or chart with each show's events scrambled, and invite the whole class to suggest the actual sequence of each show's events. Encourage the students to explain their decisions. Each of the four original smaller groups confirms or refutes the class decisions as to correct sequence. Below are two ways of organizing the sequencing and one example typical of the way that children might arrange a story drawn from TV's "Little House on the Prairie."

First	(B)	A.	Father went to look for work.	First	(B)
Second	(D)	B.	The crops were planted.	Next	(D)
Third	(A)	C.	Laura missed Father that night.	Next	(A)
Fourth	(C)	D.	A storm blew the wheat down.	Next to last	(C)
Last	(E)	E.	Father worked with a hammer.	Last	(E)

* * * * * * *

A harder version of WHAT'S NEXT may be played by selecting a story fragment in which events within one scene or within one conversation are used in a sequence experience. An example might be to order the exact sequence in a single episode of "Roadrunner." Another experience might be to retell a conversation held on "Marcus Welby." A favorite conversation to retell in sequence might be one in which Columbo is talking with a suspect. (Older children enjoyed dramatizing the Columbo scene.)

WHO IS LIKE WHAT?   Primary

Experiences: Description of character   Adapts to all ages
traits/comparison of
character relationships/
identification with characters

Teachers have been amazed to learn how much even small children have discerned about television characters. Children have shown wide knowledge about both fictional TV people as well as about the professional entertainers who play those roles. I have found value in using children's interest in TV people to help the youngsters study characterization. I have played games requiring difficult questioning processes, and found children excited and able to characterize the people they watch on TV. WHO IS LIKE WHAT? is such an experience. Its description follows:

I have enjoyed WHO IS LIKE WHAT? with primary children using a list of random characters that they suggested.

Tarzan	Laura Ingalls	John-Boy	Mr. Apple	Scooby-Doo
Grannie	Grandma Walton	Samantha	J.J.	Superman

I asked the children to tell the three most important things that describe each person. They were encouraged to explain their reasons for saying, for example, that "Tarzan is strong," and that "Grandma Walton is grouchy." They usually explained their descriptions by giving an example of what the character does, which is of course one way a person determines character traits. I then encouraged a discussion of that character's relationships with others on his show. When you have this discussion, you will probably be surprised at the comparisons the youngsters make, as well as at their understanding of various relationships.

*   *   *   *   *   *   *

A special and more difficult version of WHO IS LIKE WHAT? may be played with your students. I asked the students about characters in a way which required them to consider two or more TV characters at once, personalities not necessarily on the same program. I found children could compare and contrast the two grandmothers in the list above. They could do the same for Tarzan and Superman, Laura Ingalls and Grandma Walton. I was astounded when one six-year-old child guessed that Grandma Walton might have been a little girl at the same time that Laura Ingalls was a child. The child was inaccurate but not far wrong.

A third-grade class decided that Tarzan, Superman, and Mr. Apple would have been friends because they were "all always trying to fix something right!"

Ask your children to choose and justify which people on the list would be friends if they met somewhere. Children I heard thought nothing of having animated Superman meet live actor Tarzan in friendship. You may learn even more from these children if you ask them to tell you which character they would most like to meet, again explaining the reason for their choices.

*   *   *   *   *   *   *

Intermediate and older students might enjoy analyzing other characters, fictional or real, in a similar manner. Here are a few names sixth graders chose to consider: Mary Tyler Moore (on- and off-camera), Bob Newhart (the same), Link, Clifton, Samantha's mother, Tim Conway, Paul Lynde, Archie Bunker, Mr. Ingalls, and Columbo. Girls were interested in talking about Christie Love, Rhoda, Richard Thomas, Donny Osmond, and "MacMillan and Wife," which is indicative of their particular growth and development. Several fifth-grade girls taped a discussion about how women are currently depicted on television as shown by the female characters in popular shows. We teachers learned much from that tape about both TV and the girls. Other mini-studies included analyzing comedy characters, people who play supernatural roles, detectives, and children playing children on television. One intermediate class chose to develop a new character for "The Waltons." Their discussion about characterization of their created character resembled what it must be like when the writers for the actual program sit down to develop their "people."

* * * * * * *

Be sure to try the description and analysis of the real people who play these roles. Have the children try to infer what television personalities might really be like when not playing their well-known roles. Lively conversations develop when children suggest conflicting inferences about the private lives of television performers. One boy was motivated to write to several TV stars asking for information that would settle the dispute among his friends. The children and I really enjoyed this productive experience with characterization.

WHO SPEAKS? Intermediate

Experience: Selection of Adapts to older
        appropriate dialogue

WHO SPEAKS? provides inferential opportunities to decide appropriate conversation based on TV characterization. Just as we were once asked who spoke the lines about "the quality of mercy," so students presently can be invited to determine which TV characters could logically deliver famous quotations or well-known phrases. I was delighted when a reluctant reader in sixth grade decided that Christie Love could have delivered Langston Hughes' "Motto," (p. 98) a hip poem written long before Christie first appeared on television. You might invite students to consider a link between Laura Ingalls or John-Boy Walton and the words of Mark Twain or Robert Louis Stevenson.

* * * * * * *

In my experience, deciding what characters say or could say, as in WHO SPEAKS?, generally leads to scriptwriting (see page 66), and dramatization. I was able to observe students' dramatization of a script they had created for "Room 222." The lines they had written were so appropriate to the original TV characters that I would not have been surprised to hear their script used on the actual program.

I asked children in second grade to tell me why programs have the names they do. They gave good reasons, many literal and many imaginative. For example, they explained that the title "Chico and the Man" was chosen because the program was "mostly about a boy named Chico and the man he works for." Another explanation was that "Rhoda" was named not only because the main star is Rhoda but also because the "man who wrote it knew people would remember Rhoda from the other show." This seven-year-old child obviously had surmised that "Rhoda" would be watched as a spin-off of the "Mary Tyler Moore Show." WHY NAME is a game which provokes fine discussion.

* * * * * * *

We played another version of the title game, RENAME THE SHOW. This time I asked the children to give new and justifiable names to well-known programs. Below are some of the very reasonable responses they composed:

	Renamed
"Sanford and Son"	"Junk and Jive"; "My Funny Old Dad"
"Chico and the Man"	"Funny Friend"; "My Friend the Boss"
"Rhoda"	"Mary's Good Friend"; "Hello, New York"
"That's My Mama"	"J. J.'s Mom"
"Scooby-Doo"	"Scaredy-Dog"
"Planet of the Apes"	"Earth Number Two"; "Man and the Monkeys"
"Six Million Dollar Man"	"Impossible Man"; "Computer Man"
"Creature Feature"	"Magic Monster Movie"

* * * * * * *

Still another way to experience the title game is SHOW THE NAME. Suggest a variety of television titles you concoct or use some of those listed below. Ask the children to decide what the program might be about that it would have that name. The children I asked to do this made very good inferences about the following titles. I asked them to interpret:

"I Can Catch Everybody"
"The Tiger's Kids"
"The Flying Phantom"

My Own TV Notes:

WINNING WISER   Intermediate

Experience: Development of   Adapts to older
         thinking processes

I deplore (as do most) any of the game shows on television which use for motivation such concepts as excessive greed, emotionally charged speculation, and exploitive advertising. Nevertheless, I have made practical use of a good many other TV game programs which require, for playing, thinking processes which children need for schoolwork. For example, I have used the format of the following game programs to enhance the language experiences indicated beside each program:

"New Price is Right"	comparison; estimation
"Now You See It"	vocabulary; rapid word recognition
"Password All Stars"	definitions; rapid comprehension
"Name that Tune"	auditory recall; rapid recognition
"Match Game"	visual memory; strategy planning
"$10,000 Pyramid"	generalization; dramatization
"To Tell the Truth"	analysis, synthesis; generalization; prediction of outcome.

I found students enjoyed using TV game formats to learn thinking processes and some content. This enjoyment has been discovered by market researchers who have consequently produced home versions of some of these games.

WORD BANKER   Primary

Experience: Development of auditory   Adapts to all ages
            vocabulary

One Saturday I watched "The Superfriends'" and recorded the following words and phrases used aloud in the opening fifteen minutes of the program:

human being	normal	force	transporting
fantastic	frozen	accounts	threat
electronic	transcript	intriguing	massive
facsimile	reasonable	prison	block
X-ray vision	atomic	tackle	disappeared
diagram	particles	spacecraft	reflective
mysterious	device	antiphoton	

I am sure that I did not note all the words of such distinction that were aired because there were so many of them packed into every quickly delivered line. It would certainly be difficult for the millions of elementary school children watching to understand these difficult words, even given the many verbal and picture context clues I observed; and yet, it is likely that the program's writers intend that both some meaning and flavor be suggested in the use of such frequent specialized terms.

I decided to try WORD BANKER. I encouraged the children to try to recall at least one word per program. They were invited to help me list new words heard on TV. The result was a special dictionary which posed varied opportunities for vocabulary development. For example, a student who added a word to the list was expected to explain on which program he had heard the word and to offer a tentative explanation of its meaning. Students found themselves estimating meanings and then, with teacher-help, checking dictionaries or encyclopedias to confirm or modify their decisions.

*   *   *   *   *   *   *

I used WORD BANKER another way. Students tried to guess from which program a word was drawn. They could do this by using the definitions and by recall as well. I was fascinated that the word "computer" has been used so often on programs such as "The Six Million Dollar Man," that even very young and less-able youngsters are able to identify this word and give it some notion of meaning. This verbal ability on the part of low-achieving students surprises teachers. We all must recall how quickly assimilated into our adult vocabulary were the expressions "expletive deleted," and "would you believe . . . ," both used many times in context on the television programs we chose to watch. For more ways to use vocabulary drawn from TV in context, see CONTEXT CUE, page 33.

WORD SEARCH   Intermediate

Experience: Development of   Adapts to older primary
            specialized vocabulary

Children have long enjoyed the word search game. I found that students examining television as a medium needed to learn the particular vocabulary of the television industry. This TV version of WORD SEARCH has proved to be an entertaining and challenging experience in recognizing television terms. I do have several suggestions for you if you decide to create your own WORD SEARCH in a manner that supports good reading skills. Avoid spelling any words backward, type the puzzle in lower-case letters, and provide all terms sought after in alphabetical order. In addition, be sure to save your rough draft for a key since it takes a long time to do a WORD SEARCH after the special words are "hidden." You should use graph paper when mocking up the puzzles, and check the final puzzle carefully before presenting it to students.

Most students find WORD SEARCH a personal and engrossing challenge. If a student does have difficulty with it, however, organize a partner or team effort to continue the searching. One way to really reinforce the words is to suggest that each child say the word that he is hunting over and over silently while he is looking for and at it. Another suggestion is to give the student a marker which he may use to "organize" his viewing of lines of letters. Suggest that he check off found words as they are located.

Here is one TV WORD SEARCH I have enjoyed using:

Television Word Search

```
s i g n o f f b c d r c h a n n e l s s m a
e t p z v n k v i e w e r n e w p q p k z n
g x a a u l v i s r a v a n t l m n e e p t
m r m r p a v d q w z m t o w s e o c t v e
e l e k c a m e r a p b i u o e a s i c o n
n r b k o i j o a u n v n n r a z c a h s n
t r q j m w z l f d p v g c k n r e l b t a
v w n b m a s l r l v w s e a s o n q t n z
c r e c e i v e r o i r l r b c d e o r p g
a l b p r o g r a m r g r e p r u l j b e u
n s s q c r d m b w j b h c h i i e i l p e
c z m w i l l r e p t v m t t p k d p b i s
e v o a a u d i e n c e z z s t i o l v s t
l h k b l k m l s b w m(t e l e v i s i o n)
s t a t i o n w b r e a k j e l b z b a d m
t a l k o s p o t v e p r i m e x t i m e e
```

Television terms:

announcer	commercial	pilot	scene	sketch
antenna	cue	prime time	screen	special
audience	episode	program	script	star
camera	guest	ratings	season	station break
cancel	lights	receiver	segment	talk spot
channel	network	rerun	show	~~television~~
			sign off	video
				viewer

(WORD SEARCH solution on page 103.)

WORD SEARCH AGAIN   Intermediate

Experience: Extension of special   Adapts to older primary
       vocabulary skills   and all older ages

Variations on WORD SEARCH hold remarkable possibilities for vocabulary building. Here are but a few other versions:

Children are asked to devise their own WORD SEARCH from lists of additional TV terms **they** help compile. One list of terms from which children created WORD SEARCH read:

Many Other Channels   **101**

director	writer	producer	cameraman	boom
prerecorded	hit	special	repeat	hit
tune	flashback	news	anchorman	meteorologist
telecast	cathode	kinescope	management	editor

* * * * * * *

Television also provides many mathematical terms which may be learned and defined through word search variations. Some of the TV math terms we noted are: Eastern Standard, daylight saving, weekly, segment, serial, daily, daytime, evening, days of week, months, seasons, hours, minutes, abbreviations of time (min., sec., hr.), vertical and horizontal, to mention but a few.

* * * * * * *

Another direction for WORD SEARCH might be to look for sentences word by word in order. Sample sentences I used are:

"Devlin" is about racing.
Zira is an ape.
The Waltons are a large family.
"Karen" is a new program.

When children search for words in this way they actually use TV as a motivation to reinforce high-frequency words and practice left-to-right sequencing.

* * * * * * *

A still more difficult WORD SEARCH may be devised by using terms or descriptions of programs. The student must determine the words, show titles, or characters before beginning the WORD SEARCH. Some sample TV definitions are:

animals take over the world _____ ("Planet of the Apes")
someone tries to sell you something _____ (commercial)
program about the oldest son _____ ("The Waltons")
typed copy of story tells actors what to do and say on the program _____ (script)
machine which records television shows on film ____ (camera)
period of the day in which most viewers watch __ (prime time)

* * * * * * *

An additional comprehension aspect of WORD SEARCH is gained if you place the vocabulary on the graph paper so that the **unused** letters (which will not be circled) spell out a message. Here is part of one WORD SEARCH with a hidden message:

```
l i v e y o u t e l e v i s i o n a s p o t r e
c u e s g s c r i p t o o w r i t e r d c u e a
h i t t s e a s o n t h m o v i e i s w o r d g
b i t a m e p r o g r a m s c h a n n e l s t v
```

Television terms:

bit	programs
channels	script
cue	season
cues	spot
hit	television
live	tv
movie	writer

Solution: Television Word Search (p. 101)

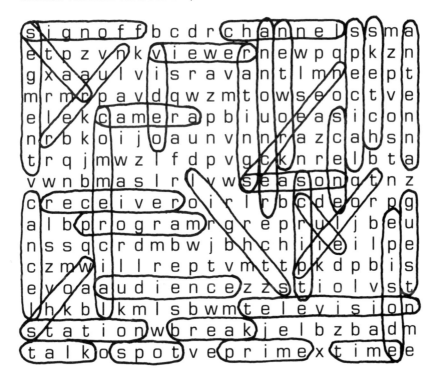

The unused letter message reads: "You are good at this word game." The message could just as easily concern the subject matter of television. Such a message just takes time and good planning—on graph paper.

WOULD-LIKE-TO-TRIES	All Ages
Experience: Creation of new experiences	Adapts to everyone

I hope that it is clear to you by now that commercial television may be used in numerous ways as a positive skill and experience builder. I have found it necessary to keep adding more channels or experiences right up to the day this manuscript was sent to the publisher, because every day teachers tell me more clever ways to use TV to help children. For example, here are just a few other experiences not discussed in this chapter, but with titles suggesting positive TV channeling. How about IDIOM, DIALECT, SPEECH FIGURES, NEWS VIEWS, PEOPLE PROBLEMS, REVIEW REVIEW, SELECTION, SPECIALS, SYNONYMS, and SYNOPSIS? I know you can devise these good experiences. Maybe you already have.

SUMMARY AND CHALLENGE

Teachers and children who have enjoyed TV experiences often think of new ways that commercial television may be used to help us learn. It is with pleasure that I leave these last several pages blank in order that you too may make your own notes and additions, perhaps inserting newly-created experiences. My only regret is that I cannot view all the new TV use ideas that you may develop and describe. Best wishes for the new season!

WOULD-LIKE-TO-TRIES

All Ages

Experience: Creation of
      new experiences

Adapts to everyone

WOULD-LIKE-TO-TRIES   All Ages

Experience: Creation of   Adapts to everyone
            new experiences

WOULD-LIKE-TO-TRIES

All Ages

Experience: Creation of
        new experiences

Adapts to everyone

The Network, the Ratings, and the New Season

TREND TOWARD TV USE

I am signing off in this chapter so that you can channel your attention to using TV experiences. I do see a trend toward using TV with children. I note three signs of change in that direction: program improvements, growth of teacher awareness, and public desire to know.

PROGRAM IMPROVEMENTS

Parents are still protesting programs for children which are scheduled past schoolnight bedtimes. They continue to be unhappy with the quantity of sugary foods promoted on children's programs. But there **are** some improvements in commercial television for children. Due to the constant attention of parental and citizen groups such as Action for Children's Television (ACT), I note that fewer TV personalities on children's programs personally promote products such as cereals, bicycles, and other toys that appeal to children. Fewer commercials interrupt children's programs. Violent elements in these children's shows have diminished somewhat. I hear about networks employing specialists in children's programming, people who are searching for more and better fare for youngsters. I have seen the introduction on Saturday morning of social, ecological, scientific, and historical themes. More specials are now offered for children.

But the really special thing I see as an improvement is that citizens' groups are themselves beginning to use television! The steadfast mothers in ACT have used their intense interest and great knowledge about television to develop what we will probably label the first TV-critical activism. They have used television to sharpen their own learning skills and responses to television. [I am fairly positive that most of us will want that kind of media literacy and comprehension to be a goal for all our children. We will undoubtedly want our children to know about and use the medium which they have always known.] If children learn to **use** television, groups such as ACT may be unnecessary in the future because many citizens will work to improve television. We can be sure that if TV literacy becomes a goal for our society, schools will be expected to help children learn these skills. I envision television, even as we know it now, as part of courses in communication, computation, career, consumer, and citizenship education.

Thanks to ACT, I will look for additional improvements in television programming for children. Thanks to ACT's own learning process, I predict a trend toward TV literacy studies in all grades as well. I am motivated to continue this looking and predicting because researchers continue to report that commercial television, as it is now, absorbs the precious interest and attention of millions of our children every day.

GROWTH OF TEACHER AWARENESS

Buried in the playground of fifty-year-old Shadowlawn Elementary (Miami, Florida) is a birthday time capsule which will be reopened in the year 2000. Onlookers at the reopening will find a television preview schedule among the many interesting items placed within the capsule by the school's faculty and students. Across the TV schedule they will see written my statement, "In the year 1974, we teachers were just beginning to realize the positive potential of commercial television." In the next paragraph I will demonstrate how true that statement may be.

When I started my television research in the early seventies, I had great difficulty locating any positive information about television at all, much less clues to its positive use. As I conclude this book

I am able to glance at the most recent educational magazines and journals and find immediate evidence of growing interest in positive TV use. Writers of recent articles are not only taking commercial television seriously, but also are starting to give us ways that we can channel TV toward education. In **Clearinghouse,** Proefriedt points out that students need to make critical evaluations of TV. He suggests that students investigate the images and values which television characters present. In **Learning** Morgan tells us some important ways TV may be used to help children study values. In a study of viewing habits reported in **Journal of Communication**, Streicher and Bonney tell us that children made discriminating decisions about commercials. Students explained how they thought television could promote learning!

Teacher is one magazine widely read by elementary teachers. Its editors have started a media column called "Amass Media," one purpose of which will be to show teachers how they can begin to integrate home TV viewing with classroom learning. In that same publication Hopkins tells us how TV and film versions of books lead to reading the books. Sterling and Cohen tell us how to use TV literary specials such as Twain's **Huckleberry Finn** to advantage in the classroom. Learning activities are suggested which help children understand their televiewing of the special.

Instructor is another magazine with a large elementary teacher circulation. This magazine boasts a regular feature called "TV News," in which fine programs are previewed and some suggestions are made for their classroom use. I find that almost every recent issue of **Instructor** had an article about TV use. I enjoyed one two-part article by Thurman and Ferguson in which they related unusual ways they had learned from the books of Laura Ingalls Wilder, the basis for TV's "Little House on the Prairie." So there are growing signs in teachers' magazines that educators are being challenged to use TV to help children learn.

The trend toward TV use is also fostered by reports of research in progress. In a recent Associated Press article (1975a) about TV serials, Mason (see also Mason) is interviewed about the preliminary findings of a massive TV-related reading experiment just concluded in Jacksonville, Florida. Mason states that the first findings seem to indicate gains in vocabulary for experimental pupils among 17,000 sixth- and seventh-grade students who were involved in special home TV serial use, classroom follow-up, and scripting. Mason declared that "people all over the country are experimenting with TV in education."

Currently I am hearing direct reports about children who lack school zeal now applying tremendous persistence on skill tasks based on popular TV shows. Teachers report increased interest in formerly reluctant learners when academic lessons were linked with television. These remarks come from teachers with students at many levels and from varied backgrounds. For example, a university friend who supervises teacher-interns reported that an intern he was visiting for the first time introduced a unit on minority groups to seventh-graders by opening a discussion about the two television programs "All in the Family," and "The Jeffersons." The students were immediately interested and participated. However, my colleague also related that while he and the intern's directing teacher were observing that lesson, they too became involved and immediately established the beginning of their own good working relationship.

PUBLIC DESIRE TO KNOW

Another way that I believe people are expressing new hope for commercial television through use is shown by the changing requests I receive for information. Two years ago even close friends were more than cautious about discussing positive TV use. Some people frankly asked me with which network I was working. People were rightly anxious about violence and television. They were wondering if I might be trying to tone down their worries about the effects of television on children. Few professional television personnel whom I contacted expressed interest in hearing about the positive results of the study inspiring this book.

POSITIVE PARENTAL POINTERS

Now things are different. I usually find that adults who hear about positive TV use become quite interested. Some are willing to discuss their own intense interest in television. Parents usually admit with some relief that they may be able to turn the tube to some advantage for both children and themselves. PTA and civic groups call me regularly for information. Local television interviewers invite me to visit. In fact as a result of PTA interest in positive television use, I have included below a list of positive parental pointers for TV use which I compiled for PTA groups. Teachers might do well to pass along these ideas to parents. In many conferences parents ask how they can help their children. Since it is at home that the constant televiewing occurs, positive TV suggestions may be among the most realistic parenting suggestions we can make. Here are some TV experiences parents have tried successfully:

1. Ask children questions about the programs they watch.
2. Help children read the TV reference material such as Sunday preview sections, newspaper schedules, and **TV Guide.**
3. Encourage selective viewing and preplanning, for example, helping students to avoid homework conflicting with TV specials.
4. Watch programs with children at least occasionally, helping them to evaluate what they view as well as noting their choices.
5. Encourage children to dictate or write letters to stars, producers, writers, and sponsors, in order to question, praise, or criticize television.
6. Entice children away from sets with other interesting and active experiences such as sports and youth organizations for a balance of interests.
7. Provide books, magazines, and newspaper articles related to favorite programs, stars, and the medium to encourage reading.
8. Discuss your dislikes with children openly and turn off set before an unfavorable program begins and attracts youngsters to it who should not see it or who should go to bed.
9. Encourage the watching of news and news commentary together, being sure to include youngsters in the discussion of the news.
10. Discuss the appeal of commercials, explaining definite resistance to unwanted products promoted on television.
11. Discuss also good products that you have bought because they were first introduced or promoted on television.
12. Take the children to a television studio. If possible let them participate on a program. Encourage them to notice and discuss the specific jobs and technical work that bring a television program to the screen.
13. Make sure that the television set does not become a standard background noise in the child's home, when no one cares to watch it.

Parents can use TV. Even the use of a few of the positive parental pointers would begin in this second generation of televiewers a far more critical appreciation of television than the one with which most of us grew up. We were the ones first fascinated. We watched anything and everything. Television was just as new to our teachers. When I look back at some of the early programs, it is easy to see why such fare may not have seemed worthy of use in school. Gradually, teachers have come to use television specials. But I am looking toward a day when we teachers will use even the worst of the programs children watch to help youngsters apply thinking skills which will in turn help them to reject such poor programs. Perhaps these students can help us recognize the truth that television is not "what the people want," but instead, "what the people haven't said they don't want." Maybe we can then work to make "television what the people really want."

UPDATING, RECYCLING, AND MINING TV

I have seen the beginning of the trend to use commercial television positively with children. In fact, in our current search for economical use of everything, we would all be missing an opportunity if we did not devise a wise use for the fantastic amount of time and interest that children have invested in television. We can recycle the wasteland that commercial television has long been assumed to be by helping children bring in their homeviewing TV observations for acceptable use in integrative classroom experiences and by planning positive use of television at school to help the student respond more wisely to television when he is again at home. Recycling might be imagined as shown on page 115.

We can reprocess TV into a clever, happy learning tool. Wouldn't it be different if we could refer to television as the "boon tube," "the keen screen," or "the mining box," all with reference to TV's potential? The potential of a mine may not be revealed at first. The true worth of television may not depend entirely on the ore in the ground, either. It may depend on how we extract and refine what resources of TV we have and how we put them to use. Of course we know that it helps to have both fine quality ore and excellent TV programs.

Not using television to the advantage of children is like losing the map of the mine and therefore the sale of the ore. No matter how good the ore is, it is worthless until you can use it. Not using TV today reminds me also of a fine book one librarian told me about that sat on a shelf in a massive library for 150 years with little use because someone left its title out of the card catalog. It really didn't matter how good the book was, we notice, since few realized its worth and used it.

SUMMARY AND CHALLENGE

We really need to prospect for better television. At the same time there seem to be good reasons why we teachers can go ahead and make positive use of commercial television as a learning alternative at school. We can begin the new season right now!

My Own TV Notes:

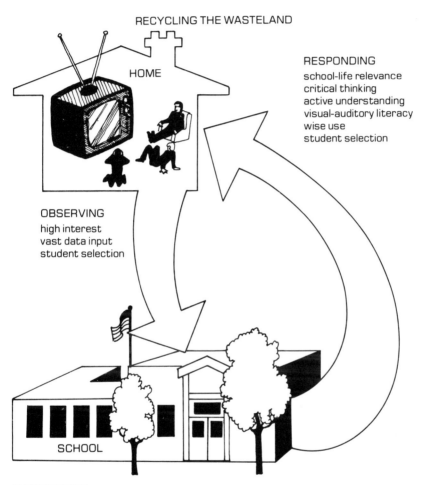

RECYCLING THE WASTELAND

HOME

RESPONDING
school-life relevance
critical thinking
active understanding
visual-auditory literacy
wise use
student selection

OBSERVING
high interest
vast data input
student selection

SCHOOL

INTEGRATING
interest
rapport
motivation
skills
child-teacher shared choice

content
values

The Scriptwriters: Sources From Period 1953-1975

Ammons, R. B. and C. H. Ammons. "The Quick Test (QT): Provisional Manual." **Psychological Reports: Monograph Supplement** 11, no. 1-8 (1969).

Associated Press. "TV and Movie Serials Aid Reading Classes in Jacksonville Program." **Miami Herald** (June 26, 1975), 1C. (a)

Associated Press. "TV Cartoons with Radio Instruction Helps Kids Increase Their Vocabulary." **Miami News** (March 18, 1975), 12A. (b)

Ball, S. and G. A. Bogatz. "A Summary of the Major Findings." **The First Year of Sesame Street: An Evaluation.** Princeton, New Jersey: Educational Testing Service, 1970.

Becker, J. **Television and the Classroom Reading Program.** IRA Service Bulletin. Newark, Delaware: International Reading Association, 1973.

Blair, M., P. Toole, and L. Laws. **Career Awareness Program.** New York: King Features Syndicate, 1971.

Blakely, R. J. "The Citizen and the Mass Media." In E. Dale (ed.), **Mass Media and Education. 53rd Yearbook National Society for the Study of Education.** Part 2. Chicago: University of Chicago, 1954, 260-86.

Bloom, B. S. (Ed.), M. D. Engelhart, E. J. Furst, W. H. Hill, and D. R. Krathwohl. **Taxonomy of Educational Objectives: The Classification of Educational Goals: Handbook 1: Cognitive Domain.** New York: David McKay Co., 1956.

Borton, T. **Dual Audio Instruction: A Broadcast Experiment.** Philadelphia: Office of Curriculum Development, Board of Education, 1972.

Borton, T. "Dual Audio Television." **Harvard Educational Review** 41 (1971) 64-78.

Breslin, D. and E. Marino. "Literacy for the '70's." **Elementary English** 51 (1974) 715-16.

Cohen, J. H. **Cool Cos: The Story of Bill Cosby.** Englewood Cliffs, New Jersey: Scholastic Book Services, 1969.

Dumas, A. **The Three Musketeers.** New York: The Heritage Press, 1953.

Fasick, A. M. A Comparative Linguistic Analysis of Books and Television for Children. Unpublished doctoral dissertation, Case Western Reserve University, Cleveland, Ohio, 1970.

Fasick, A. M. "Television Language and Book Language." **Elementary English** 50 (1973) 125–31.

Feeley, J. T. "Television and Children's Reading." **Elementary English** 50 (1973) 141–48.

Folger, S. "Progress Report On TV." **Elementary School Journal** 53 (1953) 513–15.

Furu, D. **Findings in the Shizuoka Survey: Children and Television: 1957-1959.** Tokyo: NHK Radio & Television Culture Research Institute, 1959. Cited in Takeshima et al. **Children and Television: Main Findings from Shizuoka Survey** (in 1967). Tokyo: NHK: Radio & Television Culture Research Institute, 1971.

Gattegno, C. **Towards a Visual Culture: Educating Through Television.** New York: Outerbridge & Dienstfrey, 1969.

Glushkova, Y. Deti ir televizora [Children At the Television Set] **Doshkel' nee Vospitanie,** 1970, **43,** no. 11 (1970) 66–69. (**Psychological Abstracts** 46, (1971).

Hamilton, H. "Try TV Tie-Ins." **Instructor** 84, no. 8 (1975) 67–69.

Haney, J. B. "Television: Introduction." **Instructor** 80, no. 2 (1975) 51.

Hatchett, E. L. "Cashing In On Prime Time." **Instructor** 80, no. 2 (1971) 57.

Himmelweit, H., A. N. Oppenheim, and P. Vince. **Television and the Child.** London: Oxford University Press, 1958.

Hipple, T. W. **Teaching English in Secondary Schools.** New York: The MacMillan Co., 1973.

Hook, J. N. **The Teaching of High School English.** New York: Ronald Press, 1972.

Hopkins, L. B. "Book Bonanza: Media to Books." **Teacher** 92 (1975) 26–28.

Hughes, L. Motto. **The Langston Hughes Reader.** New York: George Braziller, 1958.

Johnson, D. D. "Dolch List Reexamined." **The Reading Teacher** 24 (1971) 449–57.

Kaye, E. **The Family Guide to Children's Television.** New York: Pantheon Books, 1974.

Lyle, J. and H. R. Hoffman. **Television in the Daily Lives of Children.** Paper presented at the meeting of the American Psychological Association. Washington, D.C.: September, 1971.

Maletzke, G. **Fernschen im leben der jugend [Television and children.].** Studien und Untersuchungen durchefuhrt im Hans Bredow—Institut fur Rundfunk und Fernschen an der Universitat Hamburg, Hans Bredow—Institute, 1959. In **National Union** Catalog: Author List, 29, 125. New York: Rowman and Littlefield, 1963.

Mason, G. E. "Children Learn Words from Commercial Television." **Elementary School Journal** 65 (1965).

Mersand, J. "Teaching the Use of Television." **Journal of English Teaching Techniques** (JETT) (Spring 1973) Reprint.

Mills, L. "Don't Laugh at the Jack-in-the-Box: Teach with TV. **Teacher** 92, no. 5 (1975) 22–24.

Morgan, J. C. "Television's Children: Video and Values." **Learning** 3, no. 8 (1975) 45.

Murphy, J. and R. Gross. **Mass Media and Education.** New York: The Fund for the Advancement of Education, 1966.

Nylin, D. W. "TV or Not TV? What Is the Question?" **Educational Leadership** 28 (1970) 139.

Popham, J. (ed.) "High school on TV." **Attitude Toward School: Grades K – 12.** Los Angeles: The Instructional Objectives Exchange (P.O. Box 24095), 1970, 82–88.

Popham, J. (ed.) "Television Actors. **Measures of Self-Concept: Grades K – 12.** Los Angeles: The Instructional Objectives Exchange (P.O. Box 24095), 1970, 75–80.

Postman, N. **Television and the Teaching of English.** New York: Appleton-Century Crofts, 1961.

Potter, R. L. The Effect of a Verbal Comprehension Experience Derived from Boy-Chosen Commercial Television Programs on Verbal Comprehension of First-Grade Boys Differentiated by Entrance Age. Unpublished doctoral dissertation, University of Miami, Coral Gables, Florida, 1973.

Proefriedt, W. A. "The Teacher and TV." **Clearinghouse** 48 (1974) 510–12.

Rodgers, M. C. **New Design in the Teaching of English.** Scranton, Pennsylvania: International Textbook, 1968.

Rubinstein, E. A., G. A. Comstock, and J. P. Murray. (eds.) **Television and Growing: The Impact of Televised Violence: Summary of the Report to the Surgeon General.** (HSM 72-9086). Washington, D.C.: United States Public Health Service, 1972.

Savage, J. F. "Jack, Janet, or Simon Barsinister?" **Elementary English** 50 (1973) 133–36.

Schramm, W. L., J. Lyle, and E. B. Parker. **Television in the Lives of Our Children.** Stanford, California: Stanford University Press, 1961.

Schuller, G., M. Devai, and J. Kodar. A televizio hatasa a gyermekekre [The effect of TV on children.] **Pszichologiai Tanulmanyok** 11 (1966) 257–68. **(Psychological Abstracts 46 [1971]).**

Spiegler, C. G. **Johnny Will Read If He Wants To Read.** University of Chicago Supplementary Education Monograph 84, no. 185 (1956).

Sterling, K. and J. Cohen. "With TV: From Classics to Classroom." **Teacher** 92 (1975) 42, 44.

Streicher, L. H. and N. J. Bonney. "Children Talk About Television." **Journal of Communication** 23 (1974) 54–61.

Stumphauzer, J. S. and B. R. Bishop. "Saturday Morning Television Cartoons: A Simple Apparatus For the Reinforcement of Behavior in Children." **Developmental Psychology** 1 (1969) 763–64.

Takeshima, R., R. Tada, H. Fujioka, N. Kikuchi, Y. Muramatsu, and A. Hamade. **Children and Television: Main Findings from Shizuoka Survey** (1967). Tokyo: NHK Radio and Television Culture Research Institute, 1971.

Teachers' guides to television. New York: Broadcasting Association's Television Information Office (P.O. Box 564, Lenox Hill Station).

Thurman, E. and M. Ferguson. "On the trail of Laura Ingalls Wilder. **Instructor** 84 (1975) 78–82.

Tolkien, J. R. R. **The Fellowship of the Ring.** New York: Ballantine Books, 1965.

"TV: A Promising Tool for Teaching Reading." Newsletter of National School Public Relations Association, **Education U.S.A.** 16, no. 19 (1974) 97.

TV Guide. Radnor, Pennsylvania: Triangle Publications.

Van Allen, R. and C. Allen. **An Introduction to a Language-Experience Program.** Levels I & II. Chicago: Encyclopedia Britannica Press, 1966.

Ward, S., G. Reale and D. Levinson. "Children's Perceptions, Explanations and Judgements of Television Advertising: A Further Explanation." In Rubinstein, E. A., G. A. Comstock and J. P. Murray (eds.). **Television and Social Behavior: Reports and Papers, Television in Day-to-Day Life: Patterns of Use,** 468–90. Rockville, Maryland: National Institute of Mental Health, 1971.

Waters, C. R. "Thank God Something Has Finally Reached Him.' **TV Guide,** 22 (Jan. 19, 1974) 6–9.

Witty, P. "Children of the Television Era." **Elementary English** 44 (1967) 528–38.

Witty, P. and P. Kinsella. "Televiewing: Some Observations from Studies, 1949-1962." **Elementary English** 34 (1962) 772-79, 802.

Xerox Education Group (ed.). "Xedia: How an Informal Experiment in Screen Reading for Children May Ultimately Transform School Libraries." **Xerox Source** 1, no. 1 (1971) 15–17.

My Own List of TV Sources:

The Listings

AP